Plate I.

Plate 2.

Secrets of God

Secrets of God

WRITINGS OF
HILDEGARD
OF BINGEN

Selected and translated from the Latin by
SABINA FLANAGAN

SHAMBHALA
Boston & London
1996

Shambhala Publications, Inc.
Horticultural Hall
300 Massachusetts Avenue
Boston, Massachusetts 02115

9 8 7 6 5 4 3 2 1

First Edition
Printed in the United States of America

⊗ This edition is printed on acid-free paper that meets
the American National Standards Institute Z39.48 Standard.
Distributed in the United States by Random House, Inc.,
and in Canada by Random House of Canada Ltd

Library of Congress Cataloging-in-Publication Data

Hildegard, Saint, 1098–1179.
[Selections, English. 1996]
Secrets of God: Writings of Hildegard of Bingen/selected and
translated by Sabina Flanagan.—1st ed.
p. cm.
Includes bibliographical references and index.
Discography: p.
ISBN 1-57062-164-0 (alk. paper)
I. Flanagan, Sabina. II. Title.
BX4700.H5A25 1996   95-48805
282'.092—dc20   CIP

For W. R. P.

Contents

List of Illustrations ix

Preface xi

Introduction 1

Scivias 8

The Book of Life's Merits 39

The Book of Divine Works 62

The Natural History 89

Causes and Cures 104

The Symphonia 119

Saints' Lives 141

Correspondence 153

Select Bibliography
and Discography 179

Index 183

Illustrations

Plate 1. (front endpaper) The Redeemer: *Scivias:* Book 2, vision 1, Eibingen manuscript. © 1978 Brepols Publishers. Corpus Christianorum Continuatio Mediaevalis 43–43A.

Plate 2. (front endpaper) Judgment Day: *Scivias:* Book 3, vision 12, Eibingen manuscript. © 1978 Brepols Publishers. Corpus Christianorum Continuatio Mediaevalis 43–43A.

Plate 3. (back endpaper) The Vision of Love: *Book of Divine Works:* Book 1, vision 1. Biblioteca Statale di Lucca, ms. 1942, f. 1v. Reproduced with permission of the Ministry of Cultural and Environmental Goods.

Plate 4. (back endpaper) Love, Humility, and Peace: *Book of Divine Works:* Book 3, vision 8. Biblioteca Statale di Lucca, ms. 1942, f. 132r. Reproduced with permission of the Ministry of Cultural and Environmental Goods.

Preface

"Many people shrink from and avoid reading the books of Hildegard because she writes in such a difficult and unusual style," wrote Gebeno, prior of Eberhach, in 1220, about a generation after Hildegard's death. Gebeno's solution to the problem was to make a short selection of what he took to be the most important passages from a few of Hildegard's works. He chose them according to his particular preoccupation—the approaching end of the world.

Today, interest in Hildegard encompasses everything she wrote, from theology to natural history, her music and songs, her social and moral ideas. It also extends to the person and personality of Hildegard herself. So the selection I have made is as wide-ranging as possible within the compass of a small book. In my selection I have chosen to translate substantial passages from Hildegard's works in order to show how she develops an argument or elaborates a description. I have tried to include extracts that show her theological and scientific concerns, illustrate certain events in her life, and also display her in a variety of relationships with her contemporaries.

While attempting to render her Latin into readable English, I have not tried to reduce it to a conversational style. As Gebeno noted, Hildegard's style was distinctive and not always transparent. Indeed, I am not sure that I have always managed to capture her exact meaning. However, my aim in this anthology and translation has been to convey the spirit, if not always the letter, of Hildegard's work. To this end I have as far as possible used inclusive terms such as "humankind" and "people," where Hildegard wrote some form of the inclusive *homo,* since the word "men" no longer serves that purpose in English. Following a tradition established in Hildegard translations I have sometimes used 'Man' to refer to Adam and, by implication, the human race. Where Hildegard refers explicitly to a biblical passage I have used the translation of the Douay-Rheims version. However, in order not to overload the text with critical apparatus, I have not identified the many biblical echoes and near-quotations with which her work abounds. Such citations can usually be found in the Latin editions of her works.

Since I began my study of Hildegard almost twenty years ago, I have been assisted in numerous ways by an ever widening circle of Hildegard scholars, to whom this must serve as a general vote of thanks. In connection with the present work I wish particularly to thank Professors Albert Derolez and Peter Dronke, who kindly allowed me to consult a prepublication copy of their edition of the *Liber Divinorum Operum* (and especially Professor Derolez for assembling and forwarding the extracts from Ghent), and, somewhat closer to home, Paul Chandler, O. Carm., and Dr. Constant Mews of Melbourne, for their prompt dispatch of further much-needed texts.

Secrets of God

Introduction

When the armies of the Western crusaders waded through blood to reclaim the holy places of Jerusalem in 1099, Hildegard of Bingen was still in her cradle. More than forty years later, finally compelled to set down the visions she had long experienced, she sought recognition and support from Bernard of Clairvaux, who was then preaching the Second Crusade amid scenes of popular enthusiasm. Within a decade of her death, the German emperor Frederick Barbarossa, whom she had both praised and castigated during her lifetime, pledged himself to join the Third Crusade (in the course of which he was accidentally drowned). These bellicose events which frame Hildegard's life show one aspect of the twelfth century. They exemplify the spirit of the age as self-confident, expansionary, masculine. Yet to Hildegard this was a time of "womanly weakness," because the original spirit of the Gospels was failing, chiefly through lack of direction from the natural leaders of the Church. So Hildegard, while sharing in the general upsurge of energy, channelled it in her own distinctive directions.

Her mission—one that she undertook reluctantly and only because of the failure of those who had a duty to direct the Church—might be regarded as an internal crusade. She called for reform of the Church in the person of its leaders

1

and teachers, who were failing both to set an example to their flocks by their own actions and to instruct them in the Christian way of life. In the course of expounding her visions she covered many aspects of medieval Christian belief, often touching on what would now be considered secular knowledge as well, although for Hildegard the distinction was less apparent than it is today. Contrary to some modern perceptions of Hildegard, her thought was in many ways more conservative than revolutionary, depending on the time-honored methodology and learning of the monastic milieu in which she spent her life.

Such circumstances, together with the special nature of the visionary experiences which taught her what to say, led Hildegard to adopt the role of God's mouthpiece—a prophet for her times, rather than a mystic with an interest in contemplative prayer or unity with the godhead. It was as a prophet that she castigated wrongdoing in high and low places and sought to indicate the true way which would lead the individual and the Church to its proper reward. Because she saw her prophetic role in biblical—and medieval—terms, as one who made known the secrets of God whether they belonged to the past, the present, or the future, she felt licensed to pronounce on an extraordinary range of matters which concerned her contemporaries and are equally pressing some nine hundred years later. This activity, coupled with the originality and power of her intellect, helps explain Hildegard's amazing popularity today.

FAMILY

Hildegard of Bingen was the tenth and last child born to a noble couple called Mechthilde and Hildebert, in Bermersheim, a village near the town of Alzey in the pleasant undulating country bordering the southern bank of the Rhine not far from Mainz. The anchoress she joined in 1106 was Jutta, the daughter of Count Stephan of Spanheim. Jutta was also related to Richardis, the Marchioness of Stade, mother of the nun Richardis who was Hildegard's assistant during the writing of the *Scivias*. No doubt when Hildegard finally decided to make her writings public her self-esteem was bolstered by confidence in her position in the social hierarchy as well as the support of a network of friends and relatives (including two brothers and a nephew) within the Church. That her worldview was feudal and hierarchical rather than egalitarian is shown by her answer to Tengswich of Andernach in the *Correspondence* (see p. 157ff.).

EDUCATION

From the scant information she provides and inferences drawn from subsequent events we may conclude that Hildegard was taught by Jutta how to read and write and how to perform the *opus dei*, the daily round of prayer which formed the liturgical basis of monastic life. This practice eventually furnished Hildegard with what amounted to a reading knowledge of Latin, besides filling her mind with an invaluable stock of imagery. However, it did not amount to the formal instruction in grammar and the reading of texts that was the usual literary foundation of the male medieval student, a point Hildegard makes clear by insisting that she was taught by "an unlearned woman" and that she could not write "as the philosophers write." Later, her beloved teacher and secretary, the monk Volmar of Disibodenberg, must also have had some influence on her intellectual development (though when it came to recording her visions Hildegard claimed that his input was minimal, being confined to correcting her grammar).

THE VISIONS

According to her first biographers, the monks Godfrey and Theodorich, who drew upon information supplied by Hildegard herself, she was aware of unusual spiritual gifts at an early age, so early, in fact that she had no words to describe her experiences. However, in subsequent accounts she often explained them in terms of a great light from which came a speaking voice. The relationship between this undifferentiated light and the more complex visions in which highly colored images of mountains, buildings, composite animals, and denizens of Heaven and Hell appear as static tableaux or moving processes is not always clear. It seems, however, that such imagery often appears reflected or shadowed within the light as in a pool of water or a mirror. The relationship between Hildegard's lifelong illnesses and her visions has led some commentators to posit a particular neurophysiological basis for them. However, such a position should not be seen as reducing her spiritual or intellectual gifts to this cause alone. Not every migraine sufferer can claim Hildegard's achievements.

HILDEGARD'S PERSONALITY

Although Hildegard has left us a great volume of writing, including hundreds of letters, her personality remains elusive. This is partly because she habitually wrote not in her own person (even in the letters) but as God's mouthpiece. The selection from Hildegard's writings presented here has been chosen with the hope that readers will be able to form their own impression of Hildegard the woman. In my view, Peter Dronke has come nearest the mark when he sums her up as "daunting and eccentric; stupendous in her powers of thought and expression; lovable in her warmth and never-wearying freshness in everything she tackled."

CHRONOLOGY OF THE LIFE
OF HILDEGARD OF BINGEN

1098   Hildegard born at Bermersheim near Alzey in the diocese of Mainz.

1106   Hildegard entrusted to the care of the anchoress Jutta of Spanheim, who lived enclosed at the Benedictine monastery of Disibodenberg.

1136   Jutta died; Hildegard became head of the small convent of nuns that had developed at Disibodenberg over the years.

1141   Hildegard forced by a particularly compelling vision to start writing down what she saw and heard. This was the beginning of her first great theological work, the *Scivias*. In writing it she was assisted by the monk Volmar of Disibodenberg and the nun Richardis of Stade.

1147/8   A portion of the *Scivias* was sent to Pope Eugenius at the Synod of Trier. He declared that the work was divinely inspired and authorized her to continue recording her visions. Hildegard began to extend her circle of correspondents. She was already composing songs, later collected to form the *Symphonia*.

1150   Hildegard moved her convent to Rupertsberg, near Bingen, on the Rhine, despite opposition from the monks of Disibodenberg.

1151–8   *Natural History* and *Causes and Cures* written. Probably also the *Life of St. Rupert*.

1151   *Scivias* completed. Hildegard opposed the removal of Richardis, who had been made abbess of a convent at Bassum in Saxony. Richardis left, however, and died within a year.

1158–62   Hildegard suffered an extended illness but also undertook her first preaching tour, along the Main as far as Bamberg.

1159   Start of eighteen-year schism between the papacy and the emperor Frederick Barbarossa.

1158–63   Composition of the *Book of Life's Merits*.

1160   Second preaching tour included Metz, Krauftal, and Hördt and a public appearance at Trier.

1161–3   Third preaching tour along the Rhine, to Cologne and Werden.

1163   Commenced third part of her theological trilogy, the *Book of Divine Works*.

1165   Hildegard founded a second community at Eibingen, across the Rhine from Bingen. She continued close supervision of it until her death.

1170   *Life of St. Disibod* compiled at the request of Abbot Helenger.

1170/1   Hildegard's last preaching tour, south to Zwiefalten.

1173   Death of Volmar; conflict over his successor; Godfrey arrived from Disibodenberg and commenced the *Life of St. Hildegard.*

1173/4   *Book of Divine Works* completed.

1177   The monk Guibert of Gembloux took up position of secretary to Hildegard.

1178   Interdict placed on Rupertsberg due to the burial of a supposed excommunicate in the convent cemetery. Singing of the divine office forbidden.

1179   Interdict lifted by Archbishop Christian of Mainz. Hildegard died, 17 September.

Scivias

The *Scivias* (the title means literally "Know the ways") comprises three books or parts, containing six, seven, and thirteen visions respectively. In each case Hildegard first describes her vision (presented here in italics) and then recounts what the "voice from Heaven" tells her by way of explanation, in a manner similar to the method used by medieval exegetes to gloss written texts. The work covers a wide range of themes encompassing the Divine Majesty, the Trinity, creation, the fall of Lucifer and Adam, the entire sweep of salvation history, with special emphasis on the Incarnation, the sacraments, the virtues, and the end of the world. (Citations are to book or part, vision and—where applicable—chapter.)

In the Prologue Hildegard describes how she was instructed to make her visions public and how, after some hesitation, she began to write the *Scivias* with the support of the monk Volmar of Disibodenberg and the nun Richardis of Stade.

And behold, in the forty-third year of my life's course, when I had fixed upon a celestial vision with great fear and trembling attention, I saw a very great splendor, in which sounded a voice from Heaven, saying to me:

"O frail mortal, ashes of ashes and dust of dust, say and write what you see and hear. But since you are fearful of speaking, artless at explaining and untaught in writing, speak and write not according to human words nor following the understanding of human intelligence, nor according to the rules of human composition, but according to what you see and hear in the heavens above and in God's wondrous works. Offer them to be understood as a listener, perceiving the words of the teacher, transmits them according to the tenor of that speech, subject to his will, showing, and instruction. So, O mortal, shall you speak what you see and hear; and write such things not after your own fashion, nor that of any other human, but according to the will of Him who knows, sees, and arranges all things in the secrets of His mysteries."

And again I heard a voice from Heaven saying to me:

"Speak, therefore, these miracles and write and say the things taught thus."

It came to pass that in the eleven hundred and forty-first year of the Incarnation of God's Son, Jesus Christ, when I was forty-two years and seven months old, that the heavens were opened and a blinding light of exceptional brilliance flowed through my entire brain. And so it kindled my whole heart and breast like a flame, not burning but warming, as the sun warms anything on which its rays fall. And suddenly I grasped the underlying meanings of the books—of the Psalter, the Gospels and other catholic books of the Old and New Testaments—not, however, that I understood how to construe the words of the text or their division into syllables or their cases and tenses.

This mysterious power of secret and wonderful visions I have sensed in myself since childhood—that is, since I was five years old—up to the present time, as it is now. But I revealed it to no one except some few fellow religious who followed the same way of life. Meanwhile, up to the time that God in His grace willed the power to be manifested, I have quietly repressed it in silence.

Indeed, the visions that I see I perceive not in dreams, nor while asleep; not in ecstasy and not with my bodily eyes or external ears; I do not see them in hidden places, but I behold them openly, awake and alert, purely with the eyes and ears of the mind, according to the will of God. How this may be is difficult for people to comprehend.

But when my childhood was completed and I reached the age of perfect strength, I heard the voice from Heaven saying:

"I am the Living Light who illuminates hidden things. And as was my pleasure I have thrust the one I chose, marvelously moved, into great wonders beyond the measure of the ancients who saw many secrets in Me. But I have laid that person low on earth, so that she will not rise up in elevation of mind. The world has in her no joy or wantonness nor care concerning worldly affairs, because I have withdrawn her from pernicious boldness, having fear and trembling in all she does. She suffers in the marrow and veins of her flesh, pinched in mind and spirit, experiencing much bodily pain, so that she has no sense of security but feels entirely blameworthy. For I have hedged about the fissures of her heart, so that her mind does not elevate itself in vainglorious pride, and she feels more fear and pain in all this than joy or pleasure.

"Whence for love of Me she searched in her heart to find one who runs in the way of salvation. And she found such a one and loved him, recognizing in him a faithful man, and one like her in undertaking the work which tends toward Me. And binding him fast to her she strove by all means, through heavenly study, that My hidden mysteries might be revealed. But that same person did not seek to rise above herself, but inclined with many sighs to him whom she found, in increase of humility and intention of goodwill. You, therefore, O mortal, who receive these things not in the turbulence of deception but in the purity of simplicity for making plain the things that are hidden, write what you see and hear."

But although I heard and saw these things, because of doubt and a low opinion of myself and because of what people might say, I refused for a long time the call to write. This was not from stubbornness but from humility, until, weighed down by the scourge of God, I fell onto a bed of sickness. At last, compelled by many infirmities, with the witness of a certain noble girl of high morality and of the man whom I had secretly sought and found, as mentioned above, I set my hand to writing. When I did so, sensing, as described, the deep profundity of the explication of the books, I rose from my sickness with renewed strength, and I was just able to bring the work to a conclusion within the space of ten years.

These visions and words took place in the time of Henry, archbishop of Mainz, and Conrad, king of the Romans, and Cuno, abbot of St. Disibod, in the pontificate of Pope Eugenius.

And I heard and wrote them not according to the invention of my own or anyone else's heart, but as I saw, heard and understood them in the heavens, through the secret mysteries of God.

And again I heard the voice from Heaven saying to me: "Proclaim and write thus." [*Sc. Protestificatio*]

THE EJECTION OF LUCIFER FROM HEAVEN
AND THE FALL OF ADAM AND EVE

Then I saw as it were a very great number of clearly defined living lamps, which taking on that fiery brilliance, thus attained a most serene splendor. And behold! a lake of great width and depth appeared, having a mouth like the mouth of a pit, belching forth fiery smoke with a great stench, from which a foul cloud, extending itself, touched what looked like a vein of deceptive appearance, and in a clear region it blasted through a white cloud, which proceeded from a certain beautiful human form containing in itself many and many stars, and thus it drove forth both the cloud and the human form from that place. When that was done a most shining splendor surrounded that region and then all the Elements of the world, which had previously existed in quietness, were changed to great commotion and displayed horrible terrors. And again I heard the voice that had spoken to me before, saying:

"Those who follow God with faithful reverence and who burn in His love with worthy devotion are not fearfully distracted from the glory of supernal beatitude by any impulse of injustice. But those who falsely serve God not only fail to advance to greater things, but are cut off by a just examination from those things which they falsely believe they possess. So this *very great number of clearly defined living lamps* represents the great army of supernal spirits shining in blessed life, highly decorated and ornamented, since when they were created by God they were not carried away by pride but strongly persisted in divine love. And they, *taking on that fiery brilliance, thus attained a most serene splendor,* since when Lucifer and his followers tried to rebel against the sublime Creator, experiencing God's zeal in the fall of the

Devil and those in league with him, they put on the vigilance of divine love, while the others embraced the torpor of ignorance in not wishing to know God. How? At the fall of the Devil great jubilation was raised in these angelic spirits who had persevered with God in righteousness, since they knew with clearest sight that God remains immovable, without any change or mutability in His power, and so He cannot be overcome by any fighter. And so, burning in His love and persevering in righteousness, they spurned all dross of injustice.

"But Lucifer, who was thrust from celestial glory because of his pride, was so mighty when first created that he perceived no lack of beauty or strength in himself. So when he looked upon his beauty and considered his powerful strength he discovered pride, which encouraged him to initiate what he desired, believing that he could complete what he had begun. And seeing the place where he thought he could live, he wished to display his beauty and strength there, and said this to himself concerning God: 'I wish to shine there just as He does here.' Then all his troops assented, saying: 'What you wish we also desire.' And when, puffed up with pride, he looked to do what he had planned, the zeal of the Lord, extending itself in fiery blackness, cast him down with all his followers, so that they were made to smolder instead of shine, and were made black instead of bright as they had once been." [*Sc.* 1.2.1–2]

HOW THE DEVIL TRICKED THE FIRST MAN BY MEANS OF THE SERPENT'S DECEPTION

"From that lake a foul cloud extending itself touched what looked like a vein . . . means that from the very depths of perdition the

Devil's fraud coming forth invaded the serpent, who already intended wickedly and fraudulently to deceive mankind. How? Because when the Devil saw Man in Paradise he cried out in great horror, saying: 'Oh, who touches me in the dwelling of true beatitude?' And thus he knew that he had not yet perfected the malice he bore within himself in any other creature; but seeing Adam and Eve walking in child-like innocence in the garden of delights, he rose up greatly amazed to deceive them through the serpent. Why? Since he understood the serpent was more like him than any other creature, he intended through its treachery to accomplish secretly what he could not do openly in his own form. So when he saw Adam and Eve turn themselves, body and mind, from the forbidden tree, he himself understood that it was by divine instruction and that in the first work they began he could very easily cast them down.

"He did not know that the tree was forbidden them, but he found out by means of his baleful questions and their answers. Wherefore *in a clear region it blasted through a white cloud containing in itself many and many stars* . . . since in that pleasant place, Eve, having an innocent mind (which she had assumed from innocent Adam, bearing in her body the whole multitude of humankind shining in the preordination of God), was assailed through the seduction of the serpent for her own downfall. Why was this? Because he knew that the softness of woman could be more easily overcome than the strength of man. He also saw that Adam burned so strongly with love for Eve that if he could himself vanquish Eve, whatever she said to Adam he would do. So the Devil *drove forth both the human form and the cloud from that place*, since that same deceiver of old, casting out Eve and Adam from the seat of beatitude by his deception, sent them into the darkness of ruin. How? In other words, he seduced Eve first, so that she could get around Adam and win his assent, because she herself could more readily lead Adam to disobedience than any other creature, being made from his rib. Wherefore woman can very easily lead man astray, when he, not differing from her, readily accepts her words." [*Sc.* 1.2.9–10]

ABOUT THE DELIGHTS OF PARADISE AND SOME CONSEQUENCES OF THE FALL

"But, as you see, when Adam and Eve were expelled from Paradise *a most shining splendor surrounded that region,* since when they went out from that pleasant place because of their transgression, the power of the divine Majesty, excising from it all stain of complete contagion, fortified that place with His clarity so that it might not be touched in any way by any reverses. This also shows that the transgression that had occurred in Paradise would one day be wiped out by His clemency and mercy.

"And so *all the Elements of the world, which had previously existed in quietness, were changed to great commotion and displayed horrible terrors,* because that Creation, which had been made to serve mankind and did not feel any opposition in itself, lost that tranquility and became disturbed, bringing extreme and numerous perturbations to mankind when Man turned to disobedience, and transgressed against God. Since Man himself had bowed to lower things, so he would be held in check by it. What does this mean? Because Man rebelled in Paradise against God, therefore even Creation, which had been subjected to him, turned against him.

"But Paradise is a pleasant place, which flourishes in the freshness of flowers and herbs and the delights of all fragrances, filled with the best of perfumes and dowered with the joy of blessed souls, giving powerful moisture to the dry ground, providing a very strong force to the earth, just as the soul provides strength to the body, since Paradise itself is not overshadowed or obscured by the perdition of sinners.

"Wherefore, hear and understand me, you who say in your hearts: 'What and why are these things?' Oh, why are you so foolish in your hearts, you who are made in the likeness and image of God? How can such great glory and honor be given to you and remain without testing, as if it were a matter of nothing and emptiness? Gold must be tried in the fire and precious stones polished to make them shine, and all things of this kind must be thoroughly scrutinized. So, O foolish people, how can what is made in the image and likeness of God exist without being tried? For humankind is to be examined above all creatures, and thereby purged through all Creation. How?

"Spirit is to be tried by spirit, flesh by flesh, earth by water, fire by ice, fight by resistance, good by evil, beauty by deformity, poverty by riches, sweetness by bitterness, health by infirmity, length by brevity, hardness by softness, height by depth, light by darkness, life by death, Paradise by Purgatory, the Kingdom of Heaven by Hell, earthly by earthly things and heavenly by heavenly things. Thus mankind is tried by all Creation, that is to say in Paradise, on Earth, and in Hell and afterward gathered to Heaven. For you see openly few things of the many that are hidden from your eyes. And why do you deride the things that are right, clearly just and good among all good things before God? Why do you disdain these things? God is just, but humankind is unjust in transgressing God's precepts when it claims to be wiser than God." [*Sc.* 1.2.26–29]

CONCERNING THE CATHOLIC FAITH
AND THE WORDS OF ISAIAH

"Those who deny the Son do not worship the Father; and they do not love the Son who do not know the Father. Those who cast aside the Holy Spirit have no part of the Father or the Son; nor do they accept the Holy Spirit who do not worship the Father and the Son. Therefore unity is to be understood in the Trinity and the Trinity in unity. O mortal, can you be alive without a heart and without blood? Even so, it is not to be believed that the Father exists without the Son, or without the Holy Spirit, nor that the Son exists without the Father or the Holy Spirit, or that the Holy Spirit exists without these two. But the Father sent His Son into the world for the redemption of mankind and then drew Him back to Himself, just as a person sends out thoughts from the heart and then recalls them. Whence Isaiah speaks of the redemptive mission of God's Only-begotten, by the will of the supernal Majesty, when he says:

" 'The Lord sent a word into Jacob, and it hath lighted upon Israel' (*Is.* 9:8). Which is to say: the Lord, that is, the eternal Father, sent the Word by which all things were done, that is the Only-begotten of God, who was without beginning in time ever in the heart of the Father according to His divinity, by the mouth of the prophets into Jacob, when they faithfully announced that the same Son of God would come into the world for the salvation of humankind. So humanity, forewarned and forearmed, might prudently overthrow the

Devil and sagely turn aside from his cunning wiles. And so that Word lighted upon Israel when that same Only-begotten of God came to the deep green freshness of the Virgin where no man had entered but which maintained its flower inviolate so that He Himself, born of a virgin, might return those who did not recognize the light of truth in the false darkness of ignorance to the true way and restore unfailing salvation.

"Whence let whoever has knowledge in the Holy Spirit and wings of faith, not ignore My admonition, but perceive it in the embrace of their soul's tasting." [*Sc.* 1.4.31–32]

THE REDEEMER*

And I, not glowing with the strength of men, nor taught by their inspiration, but formed in the softness of the fragile rib, imbued with mystic breath, *saw, as it were, an incomprehensible, inextinguishable, brightly blazing fire, totally alive, and bearing the totality of life, having in itself a flame the color of air, which burnt ardently with a steady incandescence and which was as inseparably present in the bright fire as are the inward parts of a human being. And I saw that flame kindle and blaze forth. And behold! a dark round emanation of great magnitude suddenly appeared, upon which that flame beat, continually striking sparks from it until it was perfected. And so Heaven and Earth shone forth, fully formed. Then that same flame extended its glowing heat to a little clod of sticky earth which lay below, warming it, so that it was made flesh and blood and breathing on it so that a living person was raised up. When that was done, that bright fire offered the person, by means of the*

---

*See plate 1 on the front endpaper of this book.

same flame which burnt ardently with a steady incandescence, a shining white flower, suspended in that flame as a dewdrop hangs on a blade of grass. The person sniffed its perfume briefly, but did not savor it in his mouth or touch it with his hands, and, turning himself away, fell into thickest darkness from which he could not raise himself.

The darkness then began to increase and spread throughout the atmosphere. Then, in this darkness, three great stars appeared clustering together, and after them many others, large and small, shining with great splendor. And there came a prodigious star, blazing with exceptional brilliance and casting its rays toward the flame already mentioned. And on the earth a radiance like the dawn appeared. The flame was incorporated within it in a marvelous manner, yet it was not separated from that other brightly blazing fire. And thus in the radiance of the dawn the supreme Will was kindled. . . .

And I heard from the Living Fire a voice speaking to me: "Oh, you are wretched dross and a female ignorant of any teaching by earthly masters, unable to read books with philosophical understanding, but since you are touched by My light, whose fire kindles within you like the burning sun, declare, proclaim and write these, My mysteries, which you see and hear in mystical vision." [*Sc.* 2.1]

CONCERNING THE OMNIPOTENCE OF GOD

"For that *brightly blazing fire* which you see represents the omnipotent living God, who in His most clear serenity was never obscured by any wrong. He is *incomprehensible* because He cannot be divided by any division, nor can His measure be taken, nor can His essence be comprehended by any spark of a creature's understanding. And He is *inextinguishable*, since He Himself is the fullness that no limit touches, and *totally alive,* for nothing at all is hidden from Him that He does not know, and He *bears the totality of life* since all that live take their life from Him." [*Sc.* 2.1.1]

THAT THE WORD WAS INDIVISIBLY WITH THE FATHER AT ALL TIMES

"But you see that *the fire has in itself a flame the color of air, which burns ardently with a steady incandescence and which is as inseparably present in the bright fire as are the inward parts of a human being.* This means that before Creation the infinite Word was in the Father. In due course it was made incarnate, miraculously without sin or stain through the fertile sweetness of the Holy Spirit, in the ardor of Charity, in the dawn of the blessed Virgin. Now just as before taking on flesh He was indivisibly in the Father, so also after the assumption of humanity He remained inseparably in Him, since a person cannot exist without the vital movements of his inward parts. Likewise, the one and only Word can by no means be separated from His Father." [*Sc.* 2.1.3]

THE CREATION OF ADAM

"Then that same flame extended its glowing heat to a little clod of sticky earth which lay below means that when all the other creatures had been created, the Word of God, in the strong will of the Father and in the love of supernal sweetness, looked on the poor, fragile matter of the soft and tender frailty of humanity, from which both good and bad were to come, lying heavy and insensate, not yet aroused by the passionate

breath of life; *and warmed it, so that it was made flesh and blood,*
that is, infused it with the freshness of warmth, since earth
is the bodily material of humanity, nourishing it with moisture, just as a mother nurses her children; and *breathed on it*
so that a living person was raised up: since He aroused him by
heavenly virtue and marvelously drew forth a man discerning
in body and soul.

"*When that was done that bright fire offered the person, by means*
of the same flame which burnt ardently with a steady incandescence,
a shining white flower, suspended in that flame as a dewdrop hangs
on a blade of grass, since, when Adam was created, the Father,
who is the most bright serenity, gave Adam, by means of His
Word, the sweet command of shining obedience in the Holy
Spirit, adhering to the same Word in the fresh greenness of
fruitfulness; this is because the most sweet liquor of holiness drips from the Father to the Holy Spirit by means of
that same Word, producing abundant fruits, just as the pure
moisture descending on the grass makes it ready to sprout.
The person sniffed its perfume briefly, but did not savor it in his
mouth or touch it with his hands, meaning he approached the
command of the law with his intelligence, as if sniffing it,
but did not receive its full force by tasting it, nor by the
work of his hands did he fulfill it with complete blessedness.
So *turning himself away, he fell into thickest darkness, from which he*
could not raise himself—since he turned his back on the divine
precept, at the counsel of the Devil he fell into the gaping
jaws of death, because he sought God neither in faith nor in
works; whence weighed down by his sins he could not rise
to true knowledge of God until He came, who was entirely
obedient to His Father and entirely without sin." [*Sc.*
2.1.7–8]

JOHN THE BAPTIST

"And there came a prodigious star, blazing with exceptional brilliance and casting its rays toward the flame already mentioned refers to the outstanding prophet John the Baptist, shining with most faithful and serene work in his miracles and prefiguring in them the true Word, that is, the true Son of God, because he did not yield to iniquity but cast it stoutly and bravely away with works of justice." [*Sc.* 2.1.10]

THE THREE POWERS OF FLAME AS AN IMAGE OF THE TRINITY

"Now just as a flame has three qualities in its burning, so there is one God in three persons. How? For the flame consists of splendid clarity and scarlet strength and fiery heat. And it has the splendid clarity so it can shine, and the scarlet strength so it can thrive, and the fiery heat so that it can burn. Therefore, by the splendid clarity understand the Father, who by paternal piety extends His light over His faithful. And in the scarlet strength that goes with it, in which the same flame shows its power, understand the Son, who assumed His body from the Virgin, in whom divinity declared its marvels; and in the fiery strength recognize the Holy Spirit who hotly kindles the minds of believers. But where there is no splendid clarity, nor scarlet strength, nor fiery heat, then no flame can be seen; thus where neither the Father, nor the Son, nor the Holy Spirit is honored, there God is not worthily venerated.

"And just as these three aspects are recognized in a single flame, so three persons are to be understood in the Unity of Divinity." [*Sc.* 2.2.6]

THE SACRAMENT OF BAPTISM

"For at whatever time of the passing hour, and whatever age or sex the person might be, that is to say male or female, infant or aged, when they come with a feeling of devotion to baptism, I will receive them with My devout remedy. And I do not refuse the rite of infant baptism, as some false deceivers claim. They lie when they say I reject such an offering, just as in the Old Testament I did not scorn the circumcision of the infant, though he did not seek it by asking or consenting, but through his parents on his behalf.

"Therefore, those who wish to attain salvation shall fulfill in all justice the faithful promise made for them by those who received them at the sacred font. And there should be three persons in honor of the holy Trinity, that is to say the priest who sprinkles the candidates and two who offer the words of faith for them. Those who therefore are joined together in this way in the act of baptism must not mingle in carnal procreation with the one who is baptized, because they are joined to the baptized in spiritual generation. In the baptism of My Son, I, the Father, thundered, which denotes the priest giving the blessing in washing, and the Holy Spirit was seen in the form of a meek creature, which represents the man who there speaks for and teaches the one to be baptized in the simplicity of his heart; and My Son was present in the flesh to be baptized, which is symbolized by the woman standing as a gentle nurturer, on account of the most sweet incarnation of My Only-begotten. What else?

"Now just as babies are nourished bodily with milk and the food ground up for them by someone else, so they should observe the teaching and faith proposed for them in baptism in their inmost hearts. Because if they do not suck the mother's breasts or eat the food ground up for them, they will very soon die. So also if they do not receive the nourishment of their most pious mother the Church, nor retain the words of the faithful teachers that were proposed to them in baptism, they will not avoid the cruelty of the death of the soul, since they have rejected the salvation of their souls and the sweetness of eternal life. And just as when babies cannot chew earthly food with their teeth, another will grind it up for them to swallow lest they die, so it is also done when in baptism they have no words to confess Me and spiritual helpers are there to provide the food of life for them, that is the Catholic Faith, lest they be engulfed in the pit of perpetual death." [*Sc.* 2.3.31–33]

HILDEGARD'S VISION OF THE CHURCH; HOW PEOPLE LIVING A SECULAR LIFE IN THE WORLD ARE ITS ORNAMENTS

"But as you see, *another splendor like a white cloud surrounds the image of the woman [the Church] in seemly fashion from the navel downward to where it has not yet developed.* This is the secular life, which in the clarity of serene intention surrounds the Church in the reverence of just assistance, from the fullness of germinating strength as far as that extremity where she has not yet shown herself in her children. How? Because near the navel is that seedbed of life from which all humankind is procreated; whence in the Church the secular people are shown there through whom she herself is to be advanced to the full number of her orders. So kings and dukes, princes and rulers with their subjects, and also others, the rich and poor and wretched mingling with the rest of the people, are indicated there. And by all these people the Church is greatly adorned, because when the laity faithfully maintain the law of God which has been set out for them, they become great ornaments to the Church, that is to say, they embrace God with many embraces, when they obey their rulers with sincere humility and devotion and when they chastise their bodies for love of Me with almsgiving and vigils and continence and even chaste widowhood and other good and godly works. Whence those who keep the law set out for them according to My will are very dear to Me." [*Sc.* 2.5.23]

A MARRIED COUPLE REQUIRE EACH OTHER'S CONSENT IF THEY WISH TO ADOPT THE RELIGIOUS LIFE

"But if any of these wish to bear My yoke of liberty rejecting worldly things, let them come quickly to Me unless they are in the bonds of marriage, which tie they cannot rashly loose unless by the will of their spouse. How? A man cannot leave his wife or a wife her husband for this intention, unless it is the will of both parties. And then they shall both decide whether they should remain together in the world or both depart from it, since it is not possible for one foot to remain with the body and the other to be cut from it and the person still to remain healthy. So it is not fitting for a husband to remain in the world and his wife to withdraw from it, or for a wife to remain in the world and her husband flee from it, if they wish to find their reward in supernal life; because if this is done unfittingly and foolishly it will be called not a sacrifice but a depredation.

"Therefore those who are lawfully joined in carnal marriage shall live together with one accord, and one shall not foolishly separate from the other without the other's consent, or without its being arranged or indicated by ecclesiastical authority, even as it is written in the Gospel: 'What therefore God hath joined together, let no man put asunder.' (*Mt.* 19:6)." [*Sc.* 2.5.24]

CHRIST'S SACRIFICE AND MARRIAGE
TO THE CHURCH

And after these things I saw, as the Son of God hung on the cross, the figure of the woman mentioned earlier [the Church], like a shining splendor hastening forth from the ancient counsel. And she was brought to Him by means of the divine power, and, raising herself up, she was bathed with the blood that flowed from His side, and joined to Him in happy spousal through the will of the supernal Father, and nobly dowered with His flesh and blood.

And I heard the voice from Heaven saying to Him: "Let this woman, O Son, be your bride in the restoration of My people and a mother to them, renewing their souls through the salvation of spirit and water."

And as the image thus grew in strength, I saw as it were an altar which she often approached and there, devoutly looking again at her marriage portion, humbly indicated it to the supernal Father and His angels. And when the priest, clad in holy vestments, came to the same altar to celebrate the divine sacrament, I saw that suddenly a great clarity of light coming from Heaven with the assistance of the angels shone wholly round about that altar, and remained there up to the time that the priest, having completed the sacrament, departed from it. But when the gospel of peace had been recited and the offering that was to be consecrated placed on the altar, and when the priest was singing the praise of almighty God, which is "Holy, holy, holy, Lord God of Sabaoth," and thus began the mysteries of those sacraments, suddenly a shining blaze of inestimable clarity, coming from the open heavens, descended on the offering and perfused it entirely with its light, just as the sun lights up the thing it pierces with its rays. And while it was irradiated like this, it was invisibly lifted up to the secret places of Heaven and again returned to the altar, just as one draws in a breath and then lets it out again, thus it was made true flesh and true blood, although it appears in the sight of mankind like bread and wine.

And as I looked on this, images of the nativity, passion, burial, resurrection and ascension of our Savior, the Only-begotten of God, immediately appeared as in a mirror, even as they happened when the Son of God was in this world. And while the priest sang the song of the innocent lamb, "Lamb of God who takest away the sins of the world," and prepared to take the holy communion himself, the fiery brilliance returned to the heavens, and thus I heard a voice saying from the closed Heaven: "Eat and drink the body and blood of My Son, to abolish Eve's transgression, so that you can be restored to your lawful heritage." And while the rest of the people approached to take the sacrament from the priest, I saw five kinds among them. For some had shining bodies and fiery souls, while some had pale bodies and appeared dark in soul; some indeed had hairy bodies and dirty souls, steeped in the filth of human pollution; some were surrounded in body with very sharp thorns and appeared diseased in soul; some seemed bloody in body with souls like stinking corpses. But of all these, when they received the sacrament, some were lit up with a fiery splendor, while others were shadowed as with a dense cloud.

And after the completion of these sacraments, when the priest had departed from the altar, the clear light coming from Heaven, which had wholly surrounded that altar as mentioned above, was withdrawn to the secret places on high. And again I heard the voice from the heights of Heaven speaking to me:

"When Jesus Christ, the true Son of God, was hanging on the cross of His passion, the Church, joined to Him in the secrets of the supernal mysteries, was dowered with His purple blood, as she indicates when, repeatedly approaching the altar, she requests her dowry and sharply observes how devoutly her children, coming to the divine mysteries, receive it. Wherefore you see, *as the Son of God hung on the cross, the figure of the woman, like a shining splendor hastening forth from the ancient counsel, brought to Him by the divine power* means: when that innocent Lamb was raised on the altar of the cross for the salvation of mankind, the Church, in the purity of the candor of its faith and of the rest of the virtues, suddenly appearing from out of the divine secrets by the most profound mysteries, was joined in Heaven by the highest Majesty to that same Only-begotten of God. How is this? Because when blood flowed from the wounded side of My Son, then the salvation of souls arose, since that glory was given to mankind from which the Devil and his followers were cast out, when My Only-begotten, suffering worldly death on the cross, despoiled Hell and led the faithful souls to Heaven. Thereby faith began to be augmented and strengthened in His disciples and in those who sincerely followed them, inasmuch as they became the inheritors of the Heavenly Kingdom. Whence *the figure of woman raising herself up was bathed with the blood and joined in happy spousal through the will of the supernal Father* since as the strength of the passion of the Son of God was ardently flowing and raising itself miraculously to the heights of the heavenly mysteries, in the same way as the perfume of good savors wafts itself on high, the Church was thereby strengthened in pure inheritance of the eternal kingdom and was faithfully joined by the will of the most high Father to the Lord's Only-begotten. How? As the wife is subject to her husband in the obedience of willing subjection, accepting his gift of fertility within the bonds of love for the procreation of children, and raising them to be his heirs, so also the Church, joined to the Son of God in the office of humility and charity transmits the regeneration of water and spirit with salvation of souls from Him for the restoration of life, lifting them to the heavens. Whence she is *nobly dowered with body and blood,* because that Only-begotten of God confers His body and blood in most excellent glory to His faithful who are both the Church and the Church's offspring, so that they may have life in the Heavenly City through Him." [*Sc.* 2.6.1]

THE VISION OF THE VIRTUES: HEAVENLY LOVE, DISCIPLINE, MODESTY, MERCY, AND VICTORY

After that I looked and behold! as if in the middle of the shining length of the wall of the building described, there stood what looked like an iron-colored tower. It was placed on the outside of that wall, four cubits wide and seven cubits high. In it I saw five images each standing in a separate niche, over which was a domed tower. The first looked to the East, the second to the Northeast, the third to the North, and the fourth to the column of the Word of God, at whose foot the patriarch Abraham sat, and the fifth to the Tower of the

Church and to those people who ran backward and forward, building it up.

They resembled each other as follows: being each dressed in silk garments and shod in white shoes, except for the fifth, who seemed to be fully armed. The second and the third were bareheaded with flowing white locks, and without mantles. But the first, third, and fourth were dressed in white tunics. And this is how they differed from each other:

The first figure had a bishop's mitre on her head and unbound white hair. She was dressed as in a white pallium, woven with purple on its two lower edges. In her right hand she bore lilies and other flowers and in her left a palm frond. And she said:

"O sweet life, O sweet embrace of eternal life, O blessed happiness, in which the eternal rewards reside. You exist in true delightfulness so that I can never be filled or satiated with the inner joy which is in my God."

Now the second was dressed as it were in a purple tunic, standing like a youth who has not yet reached the age of full manhood, but of great seriousness. And she said: "The frightful enemy, that is, the Devil, will not terrify me from the discipline of God in whose sight I always stand, neither will human enemies, nor the world."

And the third covered her face with the white sleeve that enveloped her right hand. And she said: "O filth and impurity of this world, flee and hide yourselves from my sight, because my Beloved was born of the pure maiden Mary."

The fourth had her hair covered with a white veil in womanly fashion and was wearing a saffron-colored mantle. On her breast was the image of Jesus Christ, around which was written: "Through the bowels of the mercy of our God, in which the Orient from on high hath visited us" [Lk. 1:78]. And she said, "I always stretch out my hand to pilgrims and the poor and needy and the weak and those who mourn."

The fifth was armed, with a helmet on her head, dressed in a coat of mail and greaves and iron gauntlets, having on her left side a shield hanging from her shoulder, girded with a sword and holding a spear in her right hand. Under her feet lay a lion, with mouth agape and tongue lolling. And there were also people, some of whom were sounding trumpets, and others were drolly making a noise with players' instruments, and others were playing diverse games. And that image, at the same time as she was trampling on the lion with her feet, savagely transfixed them with the spear she carried in her right hand. And she said: "I vanquish the strong Devil and you, Hate and Envy, and you, O Filth, with your false deceiving games." [Sc. 3.3].

THE VIRTUE OF DISCRETION

The figure that sat on a stone at the end of the wall was dressed in a dark tunic. On her right shoulder she had a small cross, bearing the image of Jesus Christ, which turned now here, now there. And as if from the clouds there shone in her breast a certain brightness of great clarity, divided into many rays as the brightness of the sun is divided when it shines through many small openings in something. And in her right hand she had a little fan-shaped branch, from the top of which three little shoots blossomed forth in a wonderful manner. She also had in her lap very tiny gemstones of all kinds, which she looked at most carefully and searchingly, just as a merchant is accustomed to look carefully at his wares. And she said:

"I am the mother of virtues, always maintaining the justice of God in all things. For in spiritual warfare and secular strife, within my conscience I always wait upon my God. I do not condemn, I do not trample underfoot, I do not scorn kings, dukes, counts, and other secular rulers, who were ordained by the Author of all things. How could it be right for ashes to spurn ashes? The crucified Son of God turns His face to all, cautioning them according to His justice and mercy. And I wish to uphold His every ordinance and institution, according to His will." [*Sc.* 3.6.6–7]

IN CHRIST ALL VIRTUES WORK TOGETHER AND ARE FULLY EXEMPLIFIED

"But *in the column mentioned there is a way up from the bottom to the top by means of a ladder* signifies that all the virtues work fully in the incarnate Son of God, who left in Himself the way of Salvation so that both the small and great in faith might find in Him the appropriate step on which to place their foot in the ascent of virtues, so that they can reach the best places where the virtues can do their work. How? Virtues are gathered in the best places of the hearts of the good for His most holy work, since they complete the Son of God in His members, that is, the people He has chosen.

"So He is also the example of perfection for all the faithful who follow the law of God, spurring themselves on from good to better. For they recognize the manifestation of the true incarnation when the Son of God was truly shown in flesh, in whom is found the most faithful ascent to Heaven. On account of this *you see all the virtues of God going up and down loaded with stones for His work*, because in God's Only-begotten the most shining virtues descend in His humanity and in His divinity reach upward.

"They descend through Him to the hearts of the faithful, who with good hearts leave their own will and incline themselves to righteous deeds, just as the workman bends down to lift a stone that he will carry to the building. And they ascend again in Him when they offer to God heavenly works perfected in mankind, rejoicing, so that the body of Christ can in this way be the more quickly perfected in His faithful members. Whence they carry, as if they were stones, the winged and clear deeds that humans perform with them, for their salvation. Thus each and every action receives wings from God, by which it can raise itself above the filth of the human mind, to obtain the shining splendor by which it shines before God, for nothing can be obstructed or hidden that flows from the fountain of eternal life.

"For a fountain should not be hidden but open, that everyone who thirsts may come to it to draw water and drink. So the Son of God is not hidden or withdrawn from His elect, but manifest, preparing Himself to reward these works so He may show by just recompense what is completed on account of His will toward humankind. Therefore the faithful shall walk in faith to God and beg His mercy, and it will be given them. But by those who do not seek it will not be found, just as a fountain does not flow to those who simply know of it but are not willing to come to it. For they must come to it if they wish to draw its water. Mankind should do likewise. Let them come to God by the law made for them by Him, and they will find Him and the food of life and the water of salvation will be given them, that they will no longer hunger nor thirst.

"Wherefore the virtues *take great pains to complete the work* since they take great pains to run like rushing waters to the divine work, inasmuch as the members of Christ, shining brighter than the sun, may be joined to His head with the noblest perfection of shining acquisitions. For this reason, as you heard, they are called the strong workers of God, because they are always strenuously engaged in the good works of the faithful." [*Sc.* 3.8.13]

ABOUT THE FIVE BEASTS REPRESENTING THE PERIODS OF WORLD HISTORY

"Although all earthly things incline toward their end because the world now, with slackening strength, is at its finish and bowed beneath the burden of many travails and calamities, yet the Bride of My Son, beset in her children as much by the forerunners of the Son of Perdition as by himself, will never be overcome. Although she will be much attacked by them, rising up at the end of time stronger and more vigorous, she will become brighter and more beautiful, and so proceed to the embrace of her Beloved more sweetly and delightfully. And this is the mystical meaning of the vision you see. For *you look to the North, and behold, there stand five beasts*, which are the five most ferocious periods of temporal rule occasioned by carnal desires, never free from the stain of sin, raging among themselves.

"*One of them is like a dog, fiery but not burning,* since this period of time will have men mordant in temperament, appearing in their opinion to be like fire, but not burning with God's justice.

"*And one is like a lion of yellow color,* since that era will sustain bellicose people, moving many wars but not worried about the righteousness of God in them: because in the yellow color those kingdoms begin to incur the fatigue of debility.

"*Another is like a pale horse:* because those times will produce people lustful in the flood of sin and in their rushing pleasure passing by the operation of good virtues. And then

the heart of their kingdoms will be broken in the pallor of
their ruin, since they will have already lost the ruddiness of
fortitude.

"But the other is like a black hog, since that time will have
rulers causing black misery in themselves and wallowing in
the mire of immorality, that is to say putting behind them
the divine law by many sins of fornication and other similar
evils, and causing many schisms in the sanctity of divine
precepts.

"The last appears like a grey wolf: because that time will
have men carrying out many depredations on the powerful
and those following after them, in these rivalries showing
themselves not black or white, but grey in their craftiness.
And dividing the heads of their kingdoms, they will cast
them down: since then will come the time when many souls
are ensnared, when the error of errors will arise from Hell to
Heaven, so that the children of light will be placed on the
rack of their martyrdom, not denying the Son of God but
casting out the Son of Perdition, who will try to capture
their wills with diabolical arts.

"And these beasts are facing the West: since these failing times
will fall with the setting sun; for just as it rises and falls so
also do people, now being born and now dying." [*Sc.*
3.11.1–6]

THE SEVEN AGES OF THE WORLD

"But O you who wish to dwell in the streets of Jerusalem,
flee the Devil and adore Him who created you. For in six
days God perfected His works and on the seventh He rested
from them. What is this?

"Six days are the numbers of the six ages, and during the sixth age fresh miracles were seen in the world, as even God completed His works on the sixth day. But now the world is in the seventh age, approaching its end, just as it were the seventh day. How? The prophets have made their pronouncements; My Son has perfected My will in the world; and the gospel has been openly preached throughout it, and during the epochs completing this number and for many more years after its completion, although there is a diversity of customs among peoples, yet the world has remained well founded by Me.

"But now the Catholic faith wavers among the people and the gospel goes limping among them, and the powerful volumes that the most learned doctors explicated with great study ebb away in shameful apathy, and the food of life of the divine scriptures has been allowed to grow stale. So now I speak through a person not eloquent concerning the scriptures, nor taught by human teachers, but I who Am speak through her new secrets and many mysteries which up to now lay hidden in the books, just as a man does who first takes clay to himself and then makes forms from it according to his will.

"O fruitful teachers of good reward, redeem your souls and proclaim these words loudly and do not disbelieve them. For if you spurn them, it is not them but Me, who am the Truth, that you condemn. You should nourish My people under My law, having care up to the time that care for them is no longer needed, when all labor and all care ceases. But concerning this era, the preordained period is at hand, hastening into the time when the Son of Perdition will come. Be strong therefore and vigorous, My elect, lest you fall into the pit of perdition, but raise high the most victorious standard of these words and rush upon the Son of Perdition. For in the confusion of those ways that precede and follow the Son of Perdition, whom you call Antichrist, follow the footsteps of the One who taught you the way of truth when He appeared in the world in the flesh with great humility and without pride. Hear therefore and understand." [*Sc.* 3.11.17–19]

THE LAST DAYS AND FINAL JUDGMENT*

After this I looked: and behold! all the Elements and all Creation were set in rigorous motion. Fire, air, and water erupted and made the earth shudder; thunder and lightning crashed, mountains and woods fell, so that all living things breathed forth their life. And all the Elements were purged so that whatever had been foul in them vanished and no longer appeared. And I heard a voice sounding with the greatest amplitude through the whole earth saying: "O children of men who are lying in the earth, all rise."

And behold, human bones, in whatever part of the earth they lay, were reassembled as in a moment and clothed in flesh, and all people arose complete in their bodies of either sex, the good shining brightly and the evil appearing in blackness, so that every person's works were openly seen in them. And some of them had been signed in the faith and some had not, and some of the signed had, as it were, a golden brilliance before their faces, others like a shadow; because it was their sign.

But suddenly from the East a very great brilliance shone forth, and there in the clouds I saw the Son of Man coming in the same form He had had in the world, with open wounds and with choirs of

---

*See plate 2 on the front endpaper of this book.

angels, and sitting on a throne of flame that warmed but did not burn, and beneath Him was this great purgation of the world. And those who were signed were caught up in the air to meet Him as in a whirlwind, where I previously saw the splendor that designates the secrets of the supernal Creator, with the good separated from the evil. But He, with a gentle voice, as the Gospel tells, blessed the just in the Celestial Kingdom and with a terrible voice delivered the unjust to infernal pains, as it is written, with no questions or answers being given about their deeds, except as the words of the Gospel indicated: since whether the works of each were good or ill manifestly appeared. Those who were not signed stood afar in the northern quarter with the diabolical hordes, nor did they come to the judgment, but they all, as in a whirlwind, seeing the end, awaited His judgment and uttered bitter groans among themselves.

And thus when the Judgment was finished, the thunder and lightning and wind and storm ceased and whatever was transitory in the Elements suddenly vanished and an immense calm descended. Then the elect were suddenly rendered more splendid than the splendor of the sun and sought the heavens in great joy with the Son of God and with the blessed hosts of angels. The damned, with the Devil and his angels, went down to the infernal places with great wailing. And thus Heaven received the elect and Hell engulfed the damned. And suddenly such great joy and praises were raised in Heaven and such sadness and wailing in Hell—surpassing all human expression. And soon all the Elements shone forth with greatest clarity as if a very dark membrane had been removed from them, so that fire no longer had its fury, nor air its humidity, nor water its ferocity, nor earth its fragility. The sun, moon, and stars shone in the firmament with great beauty and splendor like so many jewels, and remained fixed in their orbits, so that they no longer told day from night. And thus there was no more night, but day. And it was finished. [Sc. 3.12]

The Book of Life's Merits

Somewhat simpler in structure than the *Scivias*, the six visions of the *Book of Life's Merits* are all variations on the immense figure of a man superimposed on the world, reaching from the heavens to the abyss, who observes in wind and clouds the various interactions of the powers of light and darkness. The distinction between the vision and the explanatory words from Heaven is not always as clearly drawn as in the *Scivias*, and the explication is often at some distance from the original sighting. In all, thirty-five vices are described, together with the virtues that oppose them. Instruction is also given about penance, confession, the uses of purgatory, and the fate of the soul after death and at the Last Judgment. (Citations are to vision or part and chapter.)

THE VISION OF THE COSMIC MAN

And I saw a man so tall that he reached from the highest clouds of Heaven to the abyss. His head and shoulders were above the clouds in the purest ether, and from his shoulders down to his thighs he was beneath these clouds in another white cloud; from his thighs to his knees he was in the earth's air. From his knees to his calves he was in the earth, and from his calves down to the soles of his feet, in the waters of the abyss on which he stood. And he had turned himself to the east so that he could look east and south.

His countenance shone with such brightness that I was not able to

39

*see it properly. There was a white cloud at his mouth which was like
a trumpet swiftly sounding with all kinds of sounds. And when the
man blew on it three winds came forth, one of which had above it a
fiery cloud, one a turbulent cloud, and one a bright cloud, so that each
wind sustained a cloud. Now the wind that had the fiery cloud above
it remained before the face of the man, while the two others with their
clouds descended to his chest and there expanded themselves; but the
wind that remained before his face with its cloud extended from the
East to the South.*

*And in the fiery cloud was a living fiery multitude who were all
joined in one accord and one life. And before them a tablet was extended, full of feathers on every side, which flew in the precepts of the
Lord. And when the precepts of God lifted the tablet on which the
knowledge of God had written certain secrets, this multitude gazed
upon them with great attention. And when they looked upon the writings, the might of God gave them the power to resound with all kinds
of music in one sound as of a very loud trumpet. [LVM 1]*

THE APPEARANCE AND WORDS OF
LOVE OF THE WORLD AND THE REPLY
OF HEAVENLY LOVE

*The first image was in human form and black like an Ethiopian,
standing naked. It had wrapped its arms and legs around a tree
below the branches, in which all kinds of varieties of flowers had
blossomed. And it gathered the flowers in its hands, saying: "I possess
all the kingdoms of the earth with their flowers and adornments. And
why should I dry up when I have all this fresh greenness? Why should
I live as if I were old when I am in the flower of youth? Why should
I turn the beautiful sight of the eyes to blindness? If I were to do that
I would be ashamed. I will gladly hold onto the beauty of this world*

for as long as I can. I do not know another life, although I hear all manner of stories about it." When these things were said, the tree withered at the roots and fell into the darkness mentioned, and the image fell with it.

And from that turbulent cloud already mentioned, I heard a voice replying to this figure: "You are very stupid because you desire to have life in the glowing embers and not seek that life which in the beauty of youth will never grow dry, and which will never decline in old age. So you lack all light, and are in black darkness; and you are cocooned in human willfulness like a worm. You also live as it were for a moment and afterward dry up like straw, and thus fall into the lake of perdition, and there you will expire in all your embraces, which you are disposed to call flowers. But I am the column of celestial harmony, and I observe all the joys of life. I do not repudiate life, but I trample underfoot all nastiness, just as I condemn you. I am the mirror of all virtues, in which each of the faithful will clearly see themselves. But you run in dark ways and your hands work disobedience." [LVM 1.1–2]

Concerning Perseverance and Holiness

"And where you see *the wind that has the turbulent cloud above it extend the cloud and itself from the South to the West,* this is because Justice, enduring with many tribulations the turbulent deeds of men, draws them with her from the South since there they burn in the perfection of faith persevering to the end, so that mankind, repudiating the Devil, may persist in good, and live in piety toward God. *And the length and breadth of this cloud is like a highway whose broad extent cannot be grasped by human minds,* since the range and spread of good works both in embracing and loving virtue is so great that their extension exceeds the mind of man.

"In the same cloud is a very great number of the blessed having all the spirits of life. No one can count them up, since those souls of the holy ones who live the blessed life reside in the blessed mansions of souls that good and holy works prepared. They are innumerable in earthly terms, as no one knows their number but God alone.

"And their voices are as the sound of many waters, since in their praises they sound like the waters of salvation, in the concord a single sound, and in the spiritual breath of a single will. They say that they had bodies but lately, as God willed, which, although turned to ashes, they still wish to have back so that they may rejoice all the more with them.

"But from those who burn in the sight of God and in His love they have the answer that they will not receive their dwellings before the divine summons and before the shaking of the Elements, when fiercest fire will purge them and God will show His great power. For the voice of God will awaken the dead, both the wicked and the elect. Then they will rise with their bodies to eternity, because their bodies will be changed to unchangeable life when they rise again, although some will receive death and some eternal life." [*LVM* 1.48–51]

THE PAINS OF PURGATORY AND PENANCE FOR LOVE OF THE WORLD

And I heard a voice from the Living Light speaking to me. "The things that you see are true and are as you see them, and there are more. For the torments of such punishments serve to purge these souls, who, while living in the transitory world, there deserved through penance the purgation of the sins from which they had not fully purged themselves in the flesh—prevented by death—and for which they were not tried by the divine scourges of a merciful God in this world. So they will be purged by these punishments, unless they are snatched from them by the pious invocation of the divine grace through people's efforts and the virtues of the saints, which God works in them.

"Those who are in the reckoning and remembrance of beatitude lose the stains of their sins through this purgation and cross to the joys of Heaven, while those who are in oblivion remain in the oblivion of other punishments.

"People who wallow in worldly love, if they wish to overcome these wicked spirits who propose love of the world to them and if they wish to avoid the punishments that you see, should castigate themselves with hair shirts and flagellation. And they should fast on plain bread and water, according to how they have sinned in desire, will, occasion, and way of life, and according to how the true Teacher, in His humanity, indicated the punishment to penitents together with confession to priests; since those who wish to do just penance should be brought before their judge, through whom the penance is placed on them according to the manner of the sin. That priest is the judge in place of My Son. Those who are accused by their consciences should present themselves to the priest for confession of their sins, in the same way as is shown in the Law concerning lepers through My servant Moses. Therefore sins should be made known to the priest, since moderate fear of confession is represented by the sweat of My Son, and penitence by the drops of His blood." [*LVM* 1.77–79]

HOW GOD SUFFERED NO LESSENING OF
POWER IN THE INCARNATION

"The book on the right wing also has two pages, since rationality in the New Testament, under the protection of supernal beatitude, shows in two ways how the one Lord God and man is manifested in the Son of God. *And one is of sapphire color and one of gold,* because virginity shone forth in Christ like the sapphire, since He Himself, born of the virginal nature, taught chastity, so all who wish to follow Him should love chastity. Whence even a golden brightness thus shines in Him, when the faithful believe Him to be the true God born of God the Father who established all things with the Father. For at the beginning of creation the Son of God was in His fullness, as He was before the ages, and He sustained no defect when He made creatures come forth, since He who was not made, made all things. Nor when He was incarnate did He know any lessening of His divinity. What you saw written on the sapphire-colored page means that the Virgin brought forth a pure man in pure virginity by a certain showing when the Lord of All sent His Word on a sweet commission to believers. So He remained in them who strove to look at God with a pure heart: and this is also written on the gold-colored page, since by an open showing and by the signs of very many miracles the Son of the World, appearing in the world, declared that He is the First Principle and that the Son of God had come, that is to say the First Principle who produced all Creation and who then, from these creatures, chose a virgin for His mother." [*LVM* 2.28]

THE DEVIL

"But that image you see like a serpent, lying supine in the darkness mentioned, shows that the Devil, that serpent of old, in the darkness of his wickedness, moves the desire of his cupidity against heavenly things when he persuades mankind to descend from heavenly desires to earthly things. *His eyes burn like fire* since the intention of the Devil emits flames in odious fire. *And his tongue hangs from his mouth* since falseness proceeds fiercely from his biting. *And his tail is cut off at the end,* since he cannot bring his works to achievement of his own will. For he wishes to draw all to the lake of perdition, if the divine Majesty did not prevent it. *His body is a black color,* because he exhorts men to total forgetfulness of God. *And there are lines of pale and evil color extending from his head downward.* This is because the ways of Satan possess the pallor of death and unleash the poisonous agitation of mankind through gluttony. So as they began their path to perdition in him, so is it prolonged in him, and they will reach a bitter end, because as the beginning of the Devil is evil, so is his end." [*LVM* 2.40]

JEREMIAH ON THE PERDITION OF SOULS

" 'How happeneth it, O Israel, that thou art in thy enemies' land? Thou art grown old in a strange country, thou art defiled with the dead: thou art counted with them that go down into Hell. Thou hast forsaken the fountain of wisdom: For if thou hadst walked in the way of God, thou hadst surely dwelt in peace forever.' (*Bar.* 3.10–13)

"The sense of which is: Whence is this evil—that you who are the manifestation of God's miracles, and will be assigned Heaven with all its shining stars where you shall see God, will be seen to be the habitation of all your enemies in that aspect whereby your mind is the land? For evil desires teem in your flesh, which are enemies of the soul. Your land began to sport in its first greenness and afterward embarked upon wantonness, and then it fell to the depths of the sea; these are squalid and lukewarm and frankly wicked works, with which your mind has grown old in a foreign land, since you commit sins, which are the opposite of holiness.

"And you do not know God, being defiled in your sleep with works of death, which stink through unbelief before God and all His saints. Wherefore you are destined for ruin with those who live in infernal torments, who do not see the day of faith nor look on the sun of mercy and who have abandoned the moon of holiness with all the stars of virtue, since they repudiated the light of all God's grace.

"And thus you have forsaken the fountain of wisdom—the life without end that is in God—which no one can ever drink dry by knowing, or understanding or seeing. For had you walked in the way of God's precepts, following Christ's footsteps, beatitude would have illuminated you and the honor of the Lord of Hosts would have led you to life, and thus you would have dwelt in the understanding of tranquil love, because God would have shown you forth before men on earth and before His angels in Heaven. He would have displayed you as the light of clarity in the renown of most holy deeds and made you ring like the sweet sound of a lyre. But because you have neglected all this you suffer calamitous disasters.

"You also, O Israel, who desire to see God in holy works,

do not imitate the lost sons of Jacob who should have denied the Devil but did not. But complete those works that God proposed to Adam in Paradise, which afterward he augmented in Abel, and which he made known in the circumcision of Abraham in the showing of the true Trinity, and which he displayed in Moses in the burning flame, and which he then made known by destroying the wicked works in the children of Israel.

"So climb the ladder of virtues that was shown to Jacob, following Christ, the Son of God, who, advancing the excellent virtues, bestows mercy on all who seek Him even as He showed in His person, when He wished to be in the world. For He himself rested in the virgin's lap like a unicorn and afterward like the horned goat ascended the mountain of virtues and miracles, by which He quite overcame the Devil and diminished his power." [*LVM* 2.51]

PUNISHMENT FOR THE MENDACIOUS

And I saw a fire burning in total blackness, in which dragons were lying who fanned the fire with their breath. And next to that fire flowed a stream of icy water, which the dragons violently agitated by entering it from time to time. But the fire and the stream had fiery air above them, which touched the fire and the stream with its heat. The souls of those who in the world practiced the vices of falsity without being forsworn and perjured were tortured in the fire and water. So they went from the heat of the fire to the cold of the water in which the dragons tormented them and from the water to the fire, but the fiery air did not harm them. However it, as well as the torments mentioned, afflicted those who fashioned falsity in their bodies through oaths and perjury. For since they had offered many falsehoods while in their bodies, they suffer that fire, and since they took pride in their excesses, they are tortured by the coldness of the water, and since they amassed them here and there they were punished by the dragons, and those who declared many falsehoods, perjured and forsworn, are burned by the air above. And I saw and understood these things. And again I heard from that Living Light a voice saying to me: "The things that you see are true, and are as you see them, and there are more." [*LVM* 2.68–69]

COMPLAINT OF THE ELEMENTS AGAINST MANKIND AND THE VICE OF PRIDE

And I saw that the man already mentioned turned himself to the North and looked north and east. And the winds and air and greenness of the world, which is under the firmament of Heaven, surrounding the man from thighs to knees, were like a garment to the man, and the fire and light of the atmosphere were like ornaments for his clothing. And from the marrow of his hipbones the powers of the Elements swelled forth, and thence returned to it, as one lets out the breath and draws it in again.

And I heard a great voice from the Elements of the world saying to that man: "We cannot run and complete our journey, as we were positioned according to our instructor. For men overturn us by their wicked deeds like a mill. Whence we stink with pestilence and the want of all justice."

But the man replied: "I will purge you with my broom, and I will try mankind repeatedly until they return to me. And in that time I shall prepare many hearts after my own heart. And as many times as you are polluted, so many times shall I purge you by tormenting the polluters.

Who can diminish me? The winds are offshoots of foulness, and the air spews forth filthiness, since people do not open their mouths to righteousness. Greenness dries up through wicked superstition of perverse crowds, which treat each particular situation according to their desires and say: 'Who is this Lord whom we have never seen?' To whom I reply: 'Do you not see Me by day and by night? Do you not see Me when you sow, and when the seed is watered by rain so that it grows? All Creation tends toward its Creator, and it understands clearly that one Person made it. Mankind, however, is rebellious and divides his Creator among many creatures. But who in His wisdom made the books? In them seek who created you. As long as Creation fulfills its function for your needs, you will not have complete joy. But after Creation falls into aridity, the elect will experience the greatest joy in the life of all joyfulness.' "

But in that cloud, in which there were a great many kinds of vices, as mentioned, I saw another seven vices in the following forms:

The first figure had a face like that of a woman with eyes of fire, a nose spattered with mud, and her mouth was closed. She had no arms or hands, but wings on each shoulder like the wings of a bat, so one wing faced the east and the other the west. And she had a man's chest to which were attached legs and feet like those of a locust, so that there was no belly or back. I could see no hair or covering of any sort on her head and the rest of her body, except that she was entirely swathed in darkness, with only a very narrow thread, like a gold circle going from the top of her head down under her chin and touching her jaw on either side. [LVM 3.1–2]

The Elements Indicate that Mankind Should Give Glory to God

"And the winds and the air and the greenness of the world, which are under the firmament of the Heaven, cover the man from his thighs to

his knees, like a garment . . . since the loft and length of the
winds and the sweet moisture of the air, and the sharp
greenness of the trees and plants, which are dependent
upon the strength of what is above, in which God is at work
producing and sustaining them, in coming forth and spread-
ing abroad, show forth His glory, when they obey Him fully
in all things. For God is glorified through the mysteries of
His creatures, just as man is honored when he is covered
over with clothing. *The fire and the brightness of the airs are*
ornaments to his garment, since the fire quickening diverse
creatures with its heat, and the light of sweetness illuminat-
ing them, honor God, as if they were to adorn Him in their
office, since He Himself is known through them, and since
by them He is named Omnipotent, inasmuch as by the shining of his garments and by the diadem on his head a man is
called lord and king.

"So also by the just deeds of souls is God glorified, because in the same way as creatures have strengths so also
does the soul. For the beginning of just desires blows in the
soul like a wind and the taste of goodwill plays over it like
the air and the completion of finished deeds flourishes in it
like the greenness of the world to advance it; and all this
is in the knowledge of the supernal secrets as if under the
firmament of the sky, since Wisdom begins to work good
deeds in the souls of the just, and the same completes it in
the soul. *And God is in these things as if from his thighs to his knees,*
since all these things that proceed from Him are also
brought to complete perfection by Him. Whence even they
are as a garment of glorification reaching from the thighs
of procreation—when good deeds are procreated in man by
God—to the knees of establishment—when they are

strengthened by God; since it is just that a person gives glory to God for his good actions and not to himself.

"But the fire of holy illumination, by which the faithful soul is lighted, lest it dry up and wither in holy works, and the light of truth, where good reputation among men is seen and heard, are like ornaments for their garments—that is to say, the glory of God—as all these things are to the glory and honor of God. For the holy soul by the just deeds which are done in the body will give glory and honor to God, since it carries them out with His help, as the prophet gives witness." [*LVM* 3.20]

PENANCE FOR BESTIALITY

"And those who are promiscuous with brute beasts so that they let their glorious human nature slip into this wicked turpitude and afterward, recognizing their outrageous crime, strive to subdue themselves by ill treatment because of it, should punish themselves with most strict fasting and very severe scourging, and let them from then on avoid the kind of beast with which they sinned, inasmuch as by penance they may outrage the Devil.

"The person who sins with brute beasts in fornication acts like one who prepares a vessel of clay and claims that this is his God, and thus dishonors God because he joins rationality with irrationality and a contrary nature. Such people are like a hard, cold stone. They are very hard because they become thus obdurate, forgetting for what honor they were created; and they are extremely cold since they extinguish the fire of the blazing Holy Spirit, when they perform this sin in most wicked blindness. Wherefore the soul, which is inextinguishable in the vessel of the body, laments when they commit that sin since it is more wicked than serpents which at least do not depart from their nature." [*LVM* 3.81–82]

How the Earth Preserves Mankind

"*And the earth in which that man was standing from his knees to his calves* contains moisture and greenness and shoots, since the earth which God kneads together by turning, pressing down and lifting up, and which He sustains by His strength, bears the moisture of the upper, inner, and lower waters, lest it crumble to dust. And earth has in it the greenness of all things that are born and flourish in youth, and of the things drawing to themselves the tinge of vigorous activity, and also the shoots of all things sprouting and sending forth the flowers of its green strength.

"And these things are like the flowering and beauty of this man's strength, and his strength is embellished by it, since when the earth produces and nourishes mankind and when it sustains and nourishes all the other things which are the servants of humanity, it appears like the flower of beauty and the embellishment of the honest virtue of God, disposing all things well and justly in His virtue.

"So also the power of God is to be honored through the earth, since she preserves humankind in all its bodily needs, who ought to praise and magnify God all the time, and since she even sustains the rest which are provided for human use, when she makes herself accessible to them for their nourishment. For when the excellence of God is praised through humanity, it is shown in just and holy works to God himself as if through the earth, from which mankind comes. And this also happens since the earth is fertile in diverse forms of generation, that is to say that all things formed among terrestrial creatures are produced from the earth, because it is like the mother of diverse offspring, both those born from the flesh and those rising up of themselves from seeds. So all things having the form and life of terrestrial creatures shall have arisen from her, since even mankind, who is animated by reason and the spirit of understanding, is made from earth.

"For earth is the material of God's work in mankind, who is the material of the humanity of the Son of God; since from earth that work was performed—that God made man—as was the matter of the Virgin who brougth forth the Son of God in pure and holy humanity without stain." [*LVM* 4.20–21]

THE VICE OF COVETOUSNESS

"For covetousness has neither love toward God, nor trusty faith toward men, but seizes and grasps all it can and freely draws others' belongings to itself, and maintains excess in mind and belly and in all its works and affairs. It is like dogs that run around everywhere and are not satisfied and like the unclean bird, which is agitated and voracious. It has dirty habits, fleeing the healthful behavior of honesty and pouring out vituperation of the many; whence it knows not God and looks to those that are alien.

"But those who flee death and love God and who seek to attain the joys of eternal salvation cast aside the excesses of covetousness and are moderate both in things that pertain to this life and to God. These things have been said concerning penitence to the souls that are to be purged and saved. And they are trustworthy, so let the faithful soul listen to them and store them up as useful knowledge." [*LVM* 4.66]

PUNISHMENT FOR THOSE WHO SOW DISCORD

And I saw others of the multitude of spirits whom I heard crying out with a great clamor: "Lucifer is our Lord, and no one, when we are with him, can overcome us." For they stir up human discord, and persuade them to be quarrelsome and to flee the harmony of the virtues.

And I saw a very great fire, next to which appeared a very dense darkness in which were worms of horrid appearance, and in which many wicked spirits ran about. And here were punished the souls of those who, when they were in their bodies, neglected the concord of holiness, and associated themselves with discord.

So they were forced to cross from that fire to the darkness mentioned, and from the darkness back again to the fire, constantly goaded by the wicked spirits. Since they had stirred up every evil through discord, they were burned in the fire; and since they caused harm to many in this way, they were tortured in the darkness; and because they were cruel, they were afflicted by the aforesaid worms; and because they made many err by these vices, they were forced to cross from the fire to the darkness and from the darkness to the fire by the wicked spirits. [*LVM* 4.67]

WORLDLY SADNESS AND HEAVENLY JOY

I saw the fifth figure in the form of a woman, at whose back a tree was standing, entirely dried up and leafless, and by whose branches the woman was entwined. For one branch went around the top of her head, and one encircled her neck and throat, and one reached around her right arm and another around her left; and her arms were not outstretched but held to herself, with her hands hanging down from the branches, and her nails were like crows' talons. From one side of her one branch came out and from the other a second which crossed around her belly and shins, and joined together. And her feet were of wood. She had no other clothes but the branches encircling her. And wicked spirits, coming with a very fetid black cloud, swarmed over her, at which she lay back lamenting.

And she said: "Alas that I was born, alas that I live! Who will help me, who will free me? If God knew me, I would not be in such great peril. Although I trust in God, He grants me no good; although I rejoice with Him, He does not lift this evil from me. I have heard many things from philosophers who teach that there is much goodness in God, but in all these things God has done no good to me. If He is my God, why does He hide all His grace from me? If He were to confer any good on me I would recognize Him. But I know not what I am. I was conceived in unhappiness and in unhappiness born and live without any consolation. Ah! what good is life without joy! And why was I created, when no good comes to me?"

But from the turbulent cloud mentioned I heard a voice giving this reply: "Oh, you are blind and deaf and do not know what you are saying within yourself. God created shining Man, but because of his prevarication the Serpent seduced him into this lake of misery. Now look at the sun and moon and the stars and all the adornments of the greenness of the earth, and think how much prosperity God gives man with these things, when man still sins with great temerity against God. You are fraudulent, sad, and impious and always rely upon Hell and do not know or understand that salvation is from God. Who gives you your part in such bright and good things but God? When day bursts upon you, you call it night; and when your salvation is present, you call it damnation; and when all your occasions and things are good, you say they are evil. So you are hellish.

"But I possess Heaven, since all that God created and which you call noxious I observe in its true light. I gently gather the blossoms of roses and lilies and all freshness in my lap when I praise all the works of God, while you attract the sorrow of sorrows to yourself since you are dolorous in all that you do. You are like the hellish spirits who always deny God in all their actions. I do not act like that; but I attribute all my works to God, since there is a measure of joy in sadness and prosperity in joy; it is not that they are like night and day. For just as God created day and night, so also are the deeds of men. For when avarice builds a castle, God immediately destroys it, and when the flesh desires wickedness, God strikes it by treading it down; and when voluptuousness of the flesh wishes vaingloriously to trace the circuits of the Heavens, God puts it to flight by striking it. Which is only right and just. For consider the nature of the birds of the air and the nastiest worms of the earth. They are at the same time useful and harmful, although they consume each other. Thus prosperity and adversity are of this world. They are not to be completely rejected, since useful things purge the harmful and the harmful purge the useful, just as gold is refined in the fire. But you take the part of the useless things, which I do not do. For I reckon up useful and useless things in the manner in which God constituted them. The soul is a witness to Heaven and the flesh is a witness to the earth. The flesh afflicts the soul, but the soul restrains the flesh. Hence consider what I say, O foolish and blind one." [LVM 5.9–11]

EXPLANATION OF THE ATTRIBUTES
OF WORLDLY SADNESS

"She had no other clothes but the branches encircling her, because this vice gives people no glory; they are adorned with no

honesty but are naked of all happiness, and as already said, show themselves oppressed by the worst calamities, since they do not love themselves or anyone else but bring heaviness to all their behavior. *The wicked spirits coming with a very fetid black cloud, at which she lay back lamenting* means that very wicked and diabolical spirits, with the blackness of their most wicked arts stirring up every filthiness and unclean sordidness, burden those people with this vice. And they drag from them all consolation and all peace of mind since they think that they themselves are desperate and abominated, and believe that no blessedness can ever come to them, just as this vice declared by her words, as shown above. But Celestial Joy replied to her and with faith urged such people to cast the bitterness of sadness from themselves, and cleave to God in joyfulness." [*LVM* 5.35]

CONCERNING WORKS OF PENITENCE

"When someone repeats a prayer in the heart by the gift of the Holy Spirit, those prayers when offered in purity cannot be hidden, but ascend to God, as He is praised both by angels and by humankind.

"For when the words of the prophets' lamentations, through which they proclaimed the justice and miracles of God, are lifted up in praise of God for the liberation from bodily affliction or for the repose of the souls of the dead, I come to aid the needs of those who mourn, because they were first uttered with sorrow and sighs. And God is the foundation of all these, and He supports them, since He is touched by them. Is not then humanity greatly loved by God, when He serves it so assiduously?

"And when people offer alms from the goods which they possess before God, God recalls the sacrifice of Abraham, and as He took pity on his son, thus He will take pity on those for whom they offer the alms, if they are worthy. For He delights in all this, since He created humanity and gave it all good things, and he does not allow it to lack anything needed, if it is fitting.

"And God gives people what they seek because of their goodwill. So goodwill is the sweetest smell to God, inasmuch as in the Old Testament God delighted not in the blood of kids but in the goodwill of humanity.

"But when people, through the gift of the Holy Spirit, impose on themselves any actions for the necessity of the living or for the repose of the dead, justly and appropriately, God accepts their hardship worthily and justly, as He heard Moses and Elijah, when they did not cease to labor for those who had sinned against God." [*LVM* 5.81–85]

The Heavenly Joys of Seculars Who Followed Christian Precepts and of Ascetics and Martyrs

And I saw an immense brightness, whose splendor was such that I could not see into it, or what was inside it unless, as it were, by looking at it in a mirror. In it I knew there was every kind of genial flowering and sweetest savors of various perfumes and very many delights. I noticed that the souls of certain of the blessed who while they lived in the fleeting world touched God with their righteous groans, and who worshipped Him with just deeds, were taking sweetest joy in all these things.

Among them I saw, as in a mirror, some who were all dressed in whitest garments; some of them had a circlet shining like the dawn on their heads, and their shoes were whiter than snow; others bore a circlet as of gold on their heads, and their shoes were shining emerald, but the rest of the adornments of these and of the others, though many, were hidden from me. For since they had renounced the Devil through faith while they were in their bodies, and since they had perfected their faith, some by fitting penance and others by good works, they attained rest in that brightness and took joy in its delightful pleasantness. And since those blessed ones, by avoiding sin and performing good works, embraced God's teachings they were dressed in white garments which Adam had cast aside.

Some of them had a circlet shining like the dawn on their heads, since through penitence they had fixed in their minds the salvation of redemption, by which God redeemed mankind, when they bewailed their sins in penitence; and since they had returned to the ways of righteousness, by the path of salvation to life, although late in the day, *their shoes appear whiter than snow.* For although they lived in a worldly manner in this life, they had made a shipwreck of their sins, before and at the hour of their death in penitence, by divine inspiration, and are thus found in salvation. Still *others,* who on account of their worldly position had not abandoned God but, living a secular life in the world though not deserting Him, willingly fulfilled His precepts in their hearts, *bore a circlet as it were of gold on their heads,* and because they had walked strongly in the laws of God, *their shoes were shining emerald.* And they, while they were in the body, did not put God behind them but devoutly fulfilled His laws and commands, although they were placed in a temporal body and in a secular life. The rest of the adornments of those and the others and what they meant were hidden from my sight and understanding.

And I saw another brightness, much greater and of infinite clarity, of which I could sense no end; and it gave off such light that I could not look upon it since it was beyond human understanding, to which that brightness already mentioned was joined, inasmuch one region extends to another, this being its beginning and origin. And in it I perceived the totality of every delight, and all kinds of music, and voices of many singers and the joy of those who rejoice, and an abundance of all gladness; for I knew in it were the souls of those saints who in this world crucified their bodies with great and hard pains and also the souls of those saints who gave their bodies over to martyrdom for the love of life; but I saw nothing of them who were in it unless as in a mirror, because I was not able to look upon such brightness.

And of those whom I saw as in a mirror, some were dressed as it were in white clouds, which appeared purer than the purest heavenly air, and as if interwoven with gold. The adornments of their heads, that is, the circlets which they had on their heads, appeared to be of amber and their shoes of crystal, giving forth a purity purer than the clearest water. And they were touched from time to time by a certain very sweet breeze, proceeding from the hidden places of God, having all the perfumes of plants and flowers; and then they gave forth the sound of sweetest harmony, and their voices resounded as the sound of many waters. The rest of their adornments, of which there were many, I could not see. Since they had apprehended God through faith with the highest and greatest devotion, and because they adored God with perfect diligence in good and most brave works, while they were living on earth, in their bodies, they are dressed in the beauty of the aforementioned clarity and take boundless delight in the joy of that brightness. Since by observing legal precepts they had fulfilled the things that are in the purity of justice, while living in this world and in the active life, *they were dressed as it were in garments of white clouds, which appear purer than the purest air,* and on account of the scrupulousness of their precepts—the precepts of His law, which they diligently observed—they shine *as if interwoven with gold.* [*LVM* 6.25–26]

DIVERSITY OF SOULS IN THE HEAVENLY KINGDOM

"Here there are, as you see, those who, renowned for serving in the body and in the burden of the world of actual life, embraced in the spirit those things that were heavenly; and those who, separating themselves from the world, in the subjection of monastic rule and in the elevation of contemplation clove body and mind to heavenly things; and those who, having subdued themselves, had ruled them kindly and humbly by teaching and example, furnishing things both corporal and spiritual; and those who, scorning idols and trusting in the Lord, did not hesitate in the constancy of truth to have their bodies weakened and brought to death; and also those who, denying they were flesh and blood and that they were human, had honestly conserved their virginity, which they had vowed to God in fear and love.

"And all these, according to how they served their Creator in good works, inspired by Him, will receive the joy of joys and the beauty of ineffable decorations. And they are blessed and will be called the blessed of My Father in the judgment of the resurrection. There they will receive much greater joy than they now have, since now they can only rejoice in their souls, but then they will have joys both of body and soul which are so unutterable that no creature shall describe them in this mortal world." [*LVM* 6.35–36]

The Book of Divine Works

This work constitutes Hildegard's most mature consideration of cosmology, salvation history, and eschatology, with particular reference to the favored place of humanity in Creation. Once more it comprises three books or parts; the first containing four visions; the second only one (the fifth) and the third, five. As well as the explication of the visions which we have come to expect, Hildegard includes some lengthy commentary on the biblical texts of Genesis 1 and the opening chapters of the Gospel of St. John. (The citation is by book, vision, and chapter.)

THE VISION AND WORDS OF LOVE*

And I saw as if in the midst of the southern airs, in the mystery of God, a beautiful and wondrous figure of human form. Its face was so beautiful and radiant that I might more easily look at the sun than upon it. A large golden ring encircled the top of its head. In the circlet above the head another face appeared, like that of an aged man, whose bearded chin touched the crown of its head. And from either side of the figure's neck wings came forth, which reached above that circlet and were joined there at the tips.

At the point where the right-hand wing curved up and backward

---

*See plate 3, on the rear endpaper of this book.

I saw the image of an eagle's head with fiery eyes, in which the brightness of angels appeared as in a mirror. At the point where the left wing curved backward was the image of a man's face, which shone like the radiance of the stars. And these faces were turned toward the East. From each of the figure's shoulders a wing swept down to its knees. And it was clad in a tunic which shone like the brightness of the sun, and in its hands it bore a lamb, shining like the light of day. It trod underfoot a monster of horrible poisonous form, black in color, and a serpent, which had its mouth clamped to the right ear of the monster, with the rest of its body curving aslant the head and its tail extending leftward to the feet.

And the image spoke thus: "I am the supreme and fiery force who has kindled all sparks of life and breathed forth none of death, and I judge things as they are. Tracing the revolving orbits with my upper wings, that is, with Wisdom, I have established true order there. I, the fiery life of the divine substance, blaze above the beauty of the fields, shine in the waters, and burn in the sun, moon, and stars.

"With the all-sustaining invisible force of the aerial wind, I bring all things to life. For the air lives in greenness and flowers; the waters flow as if living; the sun is also alive in its light, and when the moon has waned completely it takes light from the sun, as if it lived again; and the stars in their light also shine as if alive.

"I have established the pillars that uphold the entire globe; that is, those winds possessing subordinate wings—the lighter winds—which maintain the stronger with their mildness, lest they extend themselves in a dangerous manner. In the same way the body holds and protects the soul, so that it does not perish. Just as the breath of the soul holds the body together, making it strong that it might not fail, so the stronger winds animate those subject to them, that they may perform their function properly. And I, the fiery force, lie hidden in these things, and they flame forth from me, as breath continually moves a person, and as the moving flame is in the fire. And all these things are alive in their essence. They are not found in death, since I am life.

"I am also Reason, having the breath of the sounding Word, through which all Creation was made, and I have breathed on all these things, so there is nothing mortal in their nature because I am life. For I am life entire, which is not struck from stones, nor budded from branches, nor rooted in the virility of the male, but all that is living is rooted in me. For Reason is the root, and the Word sounding in truth is its flower. Now since God is reasonable, how could He not be working, when all His work flowered through Man whom He made in His own image and likeness, and in whom all Creation is represented according to his measure? From eternity it was ever God's wish to realize His work, that is to say, Man. So when He finished that work, He gave him all creatures to work with, as even God had made mankind His work.

"And since all vitality blazes forth from me, I also serve; and I am life eternally the same, without beginning or end. So the same life moving itself and working is God, and this single life has three powers. Eternity is called the Father, the Word is called the Son, and the breath connecting the two is called the Holy Spirit, just as God indicated in Man, with his body, soul, and reason.

"That I flame above the beauty of the fields, refers to the earth, which is the matter from which God made Man; and that I shine in the waters, relates to the soul; because just as water permeates the earth completely, so the soul is spread throughout the body; that I burn in the sun and moon, represents Reason; the stars are the numberless words of Reason. And that with the all-sustaining invisible force of the aerial wind I bring everything to life means: by means of the airy winds the things which grow by degrees maintain their vigor unchanged in their essential being." [*LDO* 1.1.1–2]

How the Incarnate Son of God Is Represented in the Figure of Love

"The reason the figure is *clad in a tunic which shone like the brightness of the sun* is that in Love the Son of God assumed a human body unstained by sin, like the sun in its beauty. And as the sun shines so high above the rest of Creation that it is beyond human reach, so no human understanding can conceive how the humanity of the Son of God might be, except through faith. And *in its hands it bears a lamb, shining like the light of day,* since Love in the works of the Son of God shows forth the mercy of true faith shining above all things. There it chooses martyrs, confessors, and penitents from publicans and sinners, and there it makes righteous men from unbelievers, as in the case of St. Paul, so that they can fly on the wings of the wind, that is into heavenly harmony. So Love performs its work openly and gradually, so that it lacks nothing but is perfectly complete. It is otherwise with people. For when they have the least possibility of doing anything, they can scarcely hold back until it is finished so it may be seen by others. Such people should ponder inwardly on these things, since even the bird when it comes from the egg lacks feathers and is not yet ready to fly, but after it gets feathers, it flies where it sees fit." [*LDO* 1.1.12]

HOW HUMANITY IS TO BE CONSIDERED AS A MICROCOSM

"The figure of a human person appears in the middle of this wheel, the top of whose head and the soles of whose feet touch that circle above and below, which is like tough white and shining air. From the right side the fingertips of the right hand and on the left the fingertips of the left hand were extended to the circle here and here, defining its roundness, as the figure stretched out its arms. This signifies that in the structure of the world humanity is at the center, since it is more powerful than the rest of Creation living there. Though small in stature, humankind is great in strength of soul, that is to say, in moving the head above and the feet below to the elements both higher and lower, and also in penetrating them by means of the actions to right and left that are performed with the hands, as the power to do this comes from the inner strength of the person. For as a person's body exceeds the heart in size, so even the strength of the soul exceeds the might of the body. And as the heart is hidden in the body, so the body is surrounded by the powers of the soul, which extend themselves throughout the entire world. And the faithful live in the knowledge of God, and turn to God in their necessity, both worldly and spiritual, sighing to Him in good times and in bad, since by such means devotion is ceaselessly offered to Him. For as people see creatures everywhere with their bodily eyes, so they see God everywhere in faith, and they know Him through His

creatures, understanding that He is their Creator." [*LDO* 1.2.15]

THE SEVEN PLANETS RELATED TO THE SEVEN GIFTS OF THE HOLY SPIRIT

"*Above the head of this figure seven planets are designated in turn, three in the circle of lucid fire, one in the circle of black fire beneath it, three in the circle of pure ether below,* signifying that the seven gifts of the Holy Spirit entirely surpass humanity's understanding through the three ages of the world, that is to say, before the Law, under the Law, and in the Gospel. The sun, placed in the circle of black fire below, denotes Almighty God, who alone by a just judgment fought against His enemies and overcame them in His power. The three in the circle beneath, made of pure ether, show that the three persons of the Divinity should be truly worshiped by mortals in the wholesome feeling of submission in pure penance— where they subject themselves fully to God, *so that toward his right side and under his feet the sun, in the same manner and position, signed and placed in its circle, may appear in the places mentioned;* since by displaying these gifts in the judgement of God and in the salvation of souls and in the example of good works, as indicated above, they express their meanings openly, since the judgment of God and the salvation of souls and the examples of the just urge that God should be feared and worshiped purely." [*LDO* 1.2.33]

LUCIFER, LIGHT, AND THE LOCATION OF HELL

"Indeed, God designated all the beautiful works of His strength in the first angel, and adorned him with stars and the beauty of fresh greenness and all kinds of sparkling stones, like the starry sky, and called him Lucifer, since he carried light from Him who is alone eternal. For I who Am showed my works in three regions of the world, that is to say in the East, the South, and the West. I left that fourth part in the North empty, where neither the sun nor moon shine. So Hell is in that quarter, out of bounds, having neither roof above nor floor below.

"And it is dark there, which enhances all brightness in My honor, since how is light to be known but by darkness? And how is darkness to be known unless by the radiant light of My servants? If this were not so, My power would lack fullness, as all My miracles could not be named. But now My power is full and perfect, and there is nothing lacking in My miracles.

"Thus brightness without darkness is called light. The living eye is the light, but blindness is the dark. Under these two complexions all things are known, whether they are good or bad. Through light the works of God, through darkness the banishment from God, which does not reach the light in those who do not wish to acknowledge it through pride." [*LDO* 1.4.12]

AIR FRUCTIFIES THE EARTH AS THE SOUL PRODUCES GOOD DEEDS IN THE BODY; THE SOUL WILL BE CLOTHED IN GOOD DEEDS AT THE LAST JUDGMENT

"The aforesaid breadth of the world contains air, which, sending green freshness in its strength to the earth, makes it fruitful, and it inclines these fruits to dryness when they have matured, by means of a windy coldness; but although it dries out the ground externally with this cold, it makes it lush within, so it may sprout in summer. For this reason, the Creator of all, who established the earth for His purposes, made the soul, through which humanity performs all its works, according to His own plan. Like holy Divinity, it is invisible to mankind, who is the work of God, and shall be working until the last day. But after the last day, when mortals will have become entirely spirit, holy Divinity and all spiritual things and the soul will be perfectly seen.

"So the soul is a fruitful power, which makes the entire person live by moving with it; and just as someone puts on a cloth woven from threads and wears it, the soul, putting on all these works—whether good or ill—as a garment, is covered with the deeds that it performed with the person, just as it is covered by the body in which it lives. And the good deeds, when the soul leaves the body, will appear like clothes shining in purest gold, because they are decorated with every adornment; but wicked deeds will stink on it, like a garment polluted with all filth.

"So the soul acts in the person like the air, which sends its strength to the earth to make it fruitful and produce its bounty, and which dries it out with winter's cold; however, this force preserves heat within to fructify the earth, since through the strength of the soul, childhood, adolescence, youth, and old age perform and perfect the fruits of good deeds, which decrepit age, as it were, dries up through its debility. But they are preserved in true faith for the rewards of eternal blessedness, after that person's end." [*LDO* 1.4.72]

HUMANITY CREATED IN GOD'S IMAGE; MAN AND WOMAN MADE COMPLEMENTARY— MAN REPRESENTING THE DIVINITY OF CHRIST AND WOMAN HIS HUMANITY

"And when God looked on Man, He was greatly pleased, since He had created him according to the embodiment of His image, and in His likeness, so that by the trumpet of the voice of reason he might announce all His miracles. So Man is the work of God perfected, because God is known through him, since God created all creatures for him and allowed him in the embrace of true love to preach and praise through the quality of his mind. But Man needed a helper in his own likeness. So God gave him a helper that was his mirror-image, Woman, in whom the whole human race lay hidden. This was also to be brought forth in the power of God's strength, just as the first man had been perfected in it. And the man and the woman were thus complementary, so that one works through the other, because man may not be called 'man' without woman, nor may woman without man be called 'woman.' For woman is the work of man, and man the form of woman's consolation. Neither could exist without the other. And man signifies the divinity of the Son of God, woman His humanity. And human beings sit on the judgment seat of the earth and command every creature, which exist subject to their discipline, and they rule over all created things." [*LDO* 1.4.100]

THE ORDERS OF ANGELS, AND HOW MANKIND WILL BECOME THE TENTH

"For God rules with power and authority in Heaven, and watches over the stars which take their fire from Him, and over the rest of Creation. So humanity sits on its throne, which is the Earth, and has dominion over the rest of Creation, because humankind is signed with the signs of omnipotent God.

"And these signs are the five senses of a person through which they understand and feel, in the power of God, that the Trinity should be venerated in the Unity of God and the Unity in the Trinity, through righteous faith; and this veneration is the adornment of the nine orders of angels, from which the diabolical host was expelled and fell. Man is the tenth order, which God restored in Himself in the first establishment of the lost angels, since He intended to become the man [Christ] in whose humanity is the tower, wherein walk those who are of the tenth order. Therefore, as was said before, God signified in humanity both the higher and lesser Creation. And after Adam was inspired through the breath of life, which is the soul, he arose, knew all the creatures, and embraced them in his soul with greatest love." [*LDO* 1.4.102]

The Beginning of the Gospel of St. John According to the Literal Sense

" 'And the Word was made flesh, and dwelt among us' (*Jn.* 1:14.)

"For the Word, which was eternally with God before the ages, and which was God, assumed flesh in the womb of the Virgin through the fervor of the Holy Spirit. And He put it on, in the same way that the veins, which are the fabric of the flesh and carry blood, are not themselves blood. God created humanity so all Creation might serve it. And so it was fitting for God to take on the garment of flesh in a human being. So the Word clothed itself in flesh, that is to say, that the Word and flesh were one, not however as if one were changed to the other, but that they are one in the unity of the person. And as the body is the clothing of the soul, so the soul cannot perform its function without the body. For the body is nothing without the soul, and the soul cannot operate without the body, whence they are one in a human being, and they are that human being. And so the work of God, that is to say, Man, was made in the likeness and image of God. For when the breath of God is sent to a body, that breath makes a person out of flesh. So the Word of God assumed flesh from the untilled flesh of the Virgin without any fiery heat so that the Word remains the Word and flesh remains flesh while yet being one, since the Word, which was timelessly before all the ages in the Father, did not change itself, but yet put on flesh." [*LDO* 1.4; part of chapter 105, 1. 498ff.]

THE WORKS OF THE FIFTH DAY OF CREATION AND THE WORDS OF ISAIAH SYMBOLIZING THE SPIRITUAL LIFE

" 'God also said: Let the waters bring forth the creeping creature having life, and the fowl that may fly over the earth under the firmament of heaven' (*Gn.* 1:20).

"This is to be understood as follows: God said at the advice of the Holy Spirit that spiritual gifts are to be built in the minds of individuals, and they, binding themselves to such things, should be removed from secular cares; and that these people, who are like the waters, should produce all the creeping virtues, that is, the souls living the contemplative life, and also the flying virtues, which surpass the common precepts of secular life, as for the love of God they ascend above and beyond the established righteousness of their seed.

"In such a way does the good field put forth a superabundant harvest from the seed with which it is sown, as my servant Isaiah says: 'Who are these that fly as clouds, and as doves to their windows?' (*Is.* 60:8). This should be understood as follows: Who are these who scorn earthly things and deny themselves and consider themselves as in the simplicity of the dove, and thus gaze on the Lord? Oh, how great is their reward with God, when they cast Him not behind them but worship Him with complete devotion. For God foreknew His work before all creation, and He created Heaven and Earth and between these two set the rest of Creation inasmuch as it was necessary for that creation.

"Now spiritual things are signified by the waters and corporeal things by the earth; and all that is unclean is cleansed in water, just as the body lives by means of the soul. . . .

" 'And God created the great whales, and every living and moving creature, which the waters brought forth, according to their kinds and every winged fowl according to its kind' (*Gn.* 1:21).

"God creates the great virtues in people, that is to say, integrity of the flesh and continence, through the inspiration of the Holy Spirit, removing from them all pomps and delights of the flesh through desire for the burning love of God. So they trample underfoot the delights of the flesh in themselves as if they were dead, and they strengthen in themselves all the virtues of the living soul that survive in this insecure life, so that they are not stained by unions of the human sort.

"And these are the living virtues who follow the Lamb, who was not stained by any spot of wickedness; and they are amenable to better things when they desist from marriage, which leads to care for earthly matters. These special virtues are produced in these people in various forms. One of them is chastity, another continence, to which the rest of the virtues cling, and they grow tall like a palm tree in the multitude of its kind." [*LDO* 2.5.42]

THE SEVENTH DAY OF REST AND
THE END OF THE WORLD

" 'Thus the heavens and the earth were finished and all their ornaments' (*Gn.* 2:1). Which is to be understood thus: All the heavenly works were completed, which in surpassing earthly things tend heavenward, together with the earthly things, which the need to bear the children of men occasions; and thus all that perfect beauty of heavenly works is constituted in the Church.

" 'And on the seventh day God ended his work which he had made: and he rested on the seventh day from all his work which he had done' (*Gn.* 2:2). This whole enterprise was completed in all these things; in other words, I thus defined My work in My Son, on the seventh day, in the fullness of all goodness, so that all the people of the Church, in seeing, hearing, and by studying the teachings, will know well what should be done by them according to My precepts. And all My establishment was thus made festal, so that it might be displayed in no other person but in the Son sent by Me, who completed all that I ordained through His teaching, and through His apostles worked openly what the prophets had previously seen in the shadows.

"Then the seventh day of My rest shone forth in the Church so that afterward by open action I might work nothing more in preaching, nor with signs of miracles, nor with the vision of the saints of old, but I should manifest in My Son the works of life, and many secrets, of past, present, and future; and I might warn My chosen ones most mildly to follow the incarnation of My Son, which flowered in the first seeding.

" 'And he blessed the seventh day, and sanctified it: because in it he had rested from all his work which God created and made' (*Gn.* 2:3). I blessed the seventh day in the salvation of souls, and sanctified it, when I sent My Son to be incarnated in the Virgin's womb. And I blessed and sanctified it, since in this, My day, I take great delight as in those who, like the blossoms of roses and lilies, are freed from the yoke of the Law as inspired by Me. So they begin to bind themselves freely, just as the Incarnation of My Son, which I promised before in the prophets, is not beholden to the precepts of the Law.

"And I finished working in this way in the Church, which was already perfected and fully established in its holy work just as it now shines, when My Son, who is My seventh work, proceeding from the womb of the Virgin through humanity, perfected all these things in the Holy Spirit with Me. So it is said in the Gospel: 'All power is given to me in heaven and in earth' (*Mt.* 28:18), which is to be understood as follows: 'From God the Father is given Me, who am the Son of the Virgin, all power by law of inheritance, to do in Heaven and to judge on Earth what is to be done and judged.' This does not mean that I transcend the will of My Father, but I look to Him in all things, since I am in the Father and He is in Me." [*LDO* 2.5.48]

The Vision of the City and the Volcano and the Mirror; the Clouds, Angels, and the Wind

And again I saw, as it were, a four-square apparition like a great city, walled alternately with brightness and darkness and furnished with certain mountains and figures. And I saw in the middle of its eastern region something like a great broad mountain of hard white stone, like a volcano in form, at whose summit a mirror of such bright purity shone forth that it seemed to outshine the sun. In it the image of a dove appeared with wings outspread ready to fly. And the same mirror held within many hidden mysteries and gave out a brightness of great breadth and height, in which many mysteries and many forms of diverse figures appeared.

For in that brightness, toward the southern part, a certain cloud appeared, white above and black below. Above it shone a great multitude of angels, some of which appeared fiery, some clear, and some like stars. They were moved in the wind like lighted lamps, and they were full of voices, which sounded like the sound of the sea. And the wind increased the voices in its zeal and by it sent fire into the darkness of the cloud mentioned, where it burned in the blackness without a flame, but soon it burst into flame there and made it vanish and disperse like dense smoke. And it projected it, billowing backward from the south above the mountain mentioned to the north, into an infinite abyss, from which it could no longer rise up, except to send a kind of mist along the ground.

And I heard as it were trumpets from Heaven sounding: "What is this that has fallen proud in its strength?" And then the white part of the cloud mentioned shone more brightly than it had before, and henceforth no one could stop the wind, which had cast the cloud with its three blasts into blackness. And again I heard the voice from Heaven saying: "God in His prescience knew all things, since before creatures were made in their forms He foreknew them and nothing was hidden from Him, which proceeds from Him from the beginning of the world to its end." [*LDO* 3.6.1]

Concerning the Incarnation and Different Forms of Knowledge

"And all these things are revealed by the incarnate Son of God, since those who believe in Him will be saved, and those who turn away from Him will be damned, since He came forth not from the root of the world but from the unflawed Virgin, by the will of the Father. And before the Incarnation He created all things with His Father and after His Incarnation He saved humanity whom He had made, since He took on human form without sin and redeemed through it the humanity He had created; which none other could do except the One who created mankind.

"For when Adam was His simple and shining son, he spent some time awake and asleep, inasmuch as he was fed in the spirit and through sleep refreshed his flesh. And so he was led to the changeless land of pleasure, that through his spirit he might know immortality, and not deny invisible things because of his corporeal vision. Immortal life has no clouded light, which depends on the formation of the eye, which only sees for a little time before darkness covers it again; this occurs in humans because the eye is covered by the occluding eyelid. And the pupil of the eye signifies the sight of the interior eye, which is unknown to the flesh. The eyelids are an indication of the corporeal vision, which looks outward.

"In two types of knowledge all human works are brought to perfection. For the knowledge of interior sight teaches humanity divine things, but the flesh hinders it; the occluded knowledge performs works of darkness according to the serpent's vision, which does not see the light. Whence it turns all that it can from the works of light, just as it did to Adam, when it overturned the light of living knowledge. For knowledge was like a prophecy in Adam, and it endured to the time when the Son of God was made man, so that He might elucidate it through Himself, as the sun illuminates the whole earth. And all the things that had been predicted—that is, the things described as performed before the Law and under the Law—He completed spiritually in Himself, when He offered Himself totally to the supernal Father, as it is written.

" 'Who makest the clouds thy chariot: who walkest upon the wings of the winds' (*Ps.* 103:2). The meaning of this passage is to be understood thus: Lord God, You are the One who makes the just desires of the faithful to be Your chariot, so that You reign in their hearts and direct Your ways over the words and writings of Your teachers, going beyond them, since You burn without stain and know no fault in Yourself. Wherefore clouds are also Your chariot, which You made like a ladder for Yourself, when, O Son of God, You mounted them in the garment that You assumed from the unique and most integral Virgin, whose closure no one ever opened or touched. So as dew makes its way into the earth You entered her, and You are rooted not in the root of a man but of divinity, in the same manner as a ray of the sun warms the earth, so that it can send forth its shoots. But when You came forth from her and while yet within, You were without any pain or corruption, as if You were asleep. Just as Eve was brought forth from the sleeping man and the man, uninjured, looked on her with joy, so the one and only Virgin clasped her Son to her breast with joy. And Eve was not created from the seed of man but from his flesh, since God created her with the same power by which He sent His Son into the Virgin. And thereafter none were found to be like Eve, the virgin and mother, nor Mary, the mother and virgin. In this way God took on the form of humanity, and covered His deity with it, which is visible to the angels in Heaven, His dwelling place. Whence humanity is also His dwelling place whom He created in height and breadth and depth." [*LDO* 3.7.12–13]

THE WORDS OF LOVE STANDING
BY THE FOUNTAIN*

The first figure said: "I am Love, the light of the living God. And Wisdom has performed her works with me, and Humility, which is rooted in the living fountain, is my helper, and Peace cleaves to her. And through the light which I am, the living light of the blessed angels shines, since as a ray shines from light, so this clarity shines from the blessed angels, and how could it do otherwise, since there is no light without radiance? For I have drawn humanity, who is rooted in me

---

*See plate 4 on the rear endpaper of this book.

as by reflection, inasmuch as the image of a thing is seen in water. Whence I am the Living Fountain, since all things that were done were as foreshadowed in me, and according to this reflection mankind was made with fire and water, inasmuch as I am fire and living water. Wherefore man has in his soul the power to arrange things according to his will. . . .

"My clarity overshadowed the prophets, who predicted what was to come by holy inspiration, so that in God everything He wished to do was foreshadowed before being done. But Reason sounds forth, and the sound is like thought, and the word like the deed. From the shadow this writing *Scivias* came forth by means of the form of a woman, which was but a pale reflection of strength and health, since these forces did not work in her.

"Therefore the Living Fountain is the Spirit of God, which He Himself sends in different directions in all His works, which are enlivened by it, having vitality through it just as the reflection of all things appears in water. And there is nothing that can see clearly whence it draws life but only as far as it feels by what it is moved. And as the water makes what is in it flow, so the soul is the living breath, always flowing in people. This makes them, by knowing, thinking, talking, and doing, flow, as it were.

"In the shadow, Wisdom metes out all things in equal measure lest one thing exceed another in its weight, and so nothing can be moved by another into its opposite. So she overcomes and constrains all the malice of diabolical arts, as she was before the beginning of all beginnings, and after their end will be at her strongest so that no one will be able to resist her. For she has summoned none to her aid, which lacks nothing since she was the first and the last, nor was a reply expected, as she was the first who worked on establish-

ing all things. And she in herself and through herself constituted all things piously and gently. And they shall be
destroyed by no enemy, since she sees most clearly the beginning and end of her works who composed all things fully
that all things may be ruled by her.

"Wisdom also contemplated her work, which she ordained in the shadow of the Living Water properly arranged,
when she revealed the natural powers of certain diverse
things, also the writings of *Life's Merits*, not to mention certain other profound mysteries, even by this untaught womanly form who, seeing these things in true visionary style,
was greatly enfeebled.

"But before all these things, Wisdom had drunk deeply
of the words of the prophets and the words of other wise
men and also of the Evangelists in the living fountain and
committed them to the disciples of the Son of God, so that
the streams of the Living Water might be diffused by them
throughout the world in which men might be caught like
fish in a net and brought to salvation.

"The fountain leaping on all sides is the purity of the
living God, and in it the clarity of God shines forth, in which
splendor God enfolds all things in great love. Their shadows
appeared in the leaping fountain before God ordered it to
produce them in their forms.

"And all things shone in me, Love, and my splendor
shows the formation of things, just as a shadow indicates the
form. And in Humility, who is my helper, Creation came
forth by the order of God, and in the same Humility, God
inclined Himself toward me. And so He raised in that blessedness, by which He can do all that He wills, the dry leaves
which had fallen, as He redeemed the things which He had
formed from earth, thence and after the Fall.

"For humankind is God's most perfect creation, who looks to Heaven and tramples the Earth in domination and rules all Creation, since through its soul it sees the heights of Heaven. For this reason and through the soul a person is celestial, but through the visible body that person is earthly. God therefore recruited mankind lying in the depths in humility against him who was cast from the Heavens, since when the serpent of old wished to disrupt the peace of the angels through pride, God checked it with His strong power lest the peace be harmed by the serpent's madness. For Satan, having great glory in the heights, figured in himself that he could have whatever he wished and not on account of this lose the glory of the stars. He wanted all these things, but in aspiring to everything, he lost all that he had." [*LDO* 3.8.2]

PRECURSORS OF THE LAST DAYS

"And afterward, through the teaching of the Apostles and through the virtues of the rest of the saints the times were made pure and bright until those days, which waned from their strength as if into womanly weakness. At that time all good practice, which by the grace of the Holy Spirit had been first implanted in mankind from the time of the Apostles, was led into the darkness of the traps with which the old serpent deceived the world. For the Apostles forged their teaching as if in steel, and closed it with the gates of Heaven, and in fear of God imposed a bridle on it so that it could be put into daily practice and not led into disrepute. And since they instituted their teaching according to the course of the sun, they sanctified it by abstinence from food, and through praise and prayer.

But the serpent of old tried, by looking within himself, to find out how he could destroy and extinguish this law, since he saw himself entirely trapped and since he knew by this that there would be a time of warring against the sons of men because he had turned human begetting into sin. Whence he inflamed a certain judge of royal name to the burning lust of prevarication, so that he called to himself many wicked vanities as if he worshiped them, which he even did for a time until the hand of God struck him, just as he trampled underfoot Nero and various other tyrants in all their glory.

Then the greenness of virtue dried up, and all justice fell into weakness, and even the green freshness of the earth declined in all its shoots, because the upper air had been changed to a different manner from that in which it had been made. So afterward summer would begin to display much coldness and winter much heat; and such excessive dryness and dampness, together with other signs which are the precursors that the Son of God had predicted to his disciples when they asked him what was to come before the Day of Judgment, were very often in evidence, so that many said that the Day of Judgment was imminent.

Whence the Son, speaking to the Father, says: 'In the beginning all Creation grew strongly, flourishing and flowering until the fresh greenness lessened. And the warrior saw it and said: "I know this time. But the golden number is not yet full. Look then to the mirror of My Father. In My body I feel weariness. My little ones weaken. Now remember that the fullness that was first made should not dry up. And then you had in yourselves, what your eye may never miss, until you see My body full of gems. For it wearies Me that all My members war against Me. See, Father, I show You My wounds. So now, all people, bend your knees to your Father so He may stretch out His hand to you!' "

This passage is to be understood in the following way: In the beginning, that is, before the Flood, so great was the fecundity of the earth that it brought forth its fruits without human labor, and then mankind, not having proper secular discipline or devotion to God, wallowed in the delights of earthly things. But after the Flood, as it were in the middle of time, that is, midway between the Flood and the coming of the Son of God to the world, flowers bloomed in sap and seed in ways that were different from their previous flowering, since the earth had then been steeped in the moisture of the waters and the heat of the sun.

And just as flowers multiplied their fruits beyond their past yield, so also the knowledge of humankind, increased in wisdom by the Holy Spirit, advanced to a new star, which manifested the King of Kings. And this Wisdom blazed from the fire of the Holy Spirit, through which the Word of God was made flesh in the womb of the Virgin, as that star indicated, and by which the Holy Spirit announced the deed It had performed in the Virgin's womb to the peoples. And the brightness of the flame of the Holy Spirit is the sound of the Word which created all things. For the Holy Spirit made fertile the womb of the Virgin and came in tongues of fire over the disciples of the Son of God. After these tongues of fire It performed many miracles with the disciples and with their successors.

And so that time going from strength to strength was called manly, and so it endured in bold dedication for many years. Afterward the greenness of its strength diminished and was changed to womanly weakness, putting off all justice and subject to the stupidity of human actions, since in these days man does whatever he pleases. So the Church is forsaken, like a widow who lacks the comfort of a man to look after her, since she does not have the true staff of authority on which people can rely.

But wicked hirelings greedy for money lay My little ones low in the valleys and forbid them to ascend to the hills and mountains, and they take away from them nobility, inheritance, goods, and riches. So they are like ravening wolves, who, following the tracks of the sheep, butcher those they seize and put to flight those they cannot butcher; and by this deception through the greater judges and wicked tyrants they devour My little ones." [*LDO* 3.10.7–8]

THE SLAYING OF ENOCH AND ELIJAH AND THE CONFOUNDING OF THE ANTICHRIST

"After Enoch and Elijah shall have been subjected to mortal death by the Son of Perdition, the followers of the Antichrist will rejoice greatly when they see that they are dead. But then He will resurrect them with the spirit of life and bear them up in the clouds, and their joy will be turned to fear and sadness and great wonder. For by their resuscitation and raising up, I, the All-powerful, shall prove that the resurrection and life of the dead can be contradicted by no refutation of unbelievers. For on that day when the Elements with which mankind sinned will be purged, they will also be revived from death, and restored in greater clarity than when first created, through penance, which is especially pleasing to God.

"So just as a person's entire frame is moved through repentance, so they also move the heavens with the mournful voice of penance and praise God and His cherubim completely. Then the serpent of old will be moved to greatest rage on account of this and will lead the accursed man to think that he might possess the throne from which he was cast down, inasmuch as by this the resuscitation of the aforementioned men and the memory of the Son of God may be completely expunged in men, and he will say to himself: 'In this, my son, I shall wage a greater war now than I have long been doing against Heaven, and I will work all my will through him, and neither God nor man will be able to resist this will of mine. I know and understand that I cannot be overcome. So I shall be victorious in all things.'

"And then that Son of Perdition will call a great crowd of people so they may see his glory made manifest when he tries to fly above the heavens, thinking that if anything of the Catholic faith were to remain intact, it would be completely destroyed by his ascension. But when he orders the superior Elements to sustain him in going to the heavens, in the hearing of the people standing around the words of My faithful Paul will be fulfilled, who, filled with the spirit of truth, says: 'And then that wicked one shall be revealed whom the Lord Jesus shall kill with the spirit of his mouth' (2 Thes. 2:8).

"The meaning of which is as follows: At that time the Son of Iniquity will be stripped bare and he will appear as false to all people, when he dares to presume to ascend to Heaven, since the Son of God, who condemns and saves the people, will kill him in this presumption, and He will do it with the strength, by which He, being the Word of the Father, will judge the whole world with a just judgment.

"For when that Son of Perdition rises above himself by devilish arts, he will be cast down by divine strength and a stink of pitch and sulfur will engulf him, so that the people standing around will flee to the protection of the mountains. Indeed, such great terror will seize those who see and hear it that, renouncing the Devil and his son, they will be converted to the true faith of baptism. On account of which the serpent of old, astonished and boiling inwardly, will say: 'We are confounded; from now on we will not be able to subject humanity to ourselves as we were wont to do.'" [*LDO* 3.10.35, 36]

EPILOGUE: HILDEGARD PAYS TRIBUTE TO HER HELPERS

At the time when I was working with true vision on the writing of this book with the help of a monk who was scrupulous in the observation of the Rule of St. Benedict, sadness pierced me body and soul, since I was parted from that happy man by his death, bereft in this world. For he, in the service of God, listened diligently to all the words of this vision without ceasing work and set them in order by correcting them. And he always warned me not to desist because of any bodily infirmity, but to busy myself by day and by night writing these things that had been shown to me in that vision. And so doing right up to his end, he could never have enough of the words of the vision; whence, he being dead, I cried with mournful voice to God, saying: "O my God, You had Your will of Your servant whom You gave me as a helper in these visions, now help me as You should!"

Then indeed, Ludwig, abbot of St. Eucharius in Trier, a

person most revered and wise before God and man, was moved to great mercy by my sorrow, so that through his own efforts and those of other wise men he faithfully offered me help with unfailing constancy. And since he well knew me and the above-mentioned happy man and the visions that I had previously seen, I rejoiced in tearful sighs over him as if I had received him from God. And another who came of a noble family, Wezelin, provost of St. Andrew's in Cologne, a man of honorable life and great steadfastness before God and anxious to perform good works through holy desire, heard and noted all the words of these visions with diligent attention for love of the Holy Spirit. And this blessed man both personally and through other wise men helped by consoling me in all my sorrow and desolation; and he faithfully heard and loved all the words of these visions without tiring, since they were sweeter than honey and honeycomb; and so through the grace of God, and with the help of these venerable men, the writing of this book was finished.

And I heard a voice from the Living Light, which taught me these visions, saying thus: "I shall make those who helped and consoled the simple soul writing My visions participants in the reward of this work." And I, a poor little woman, taught by the vision, said: "My God, grant to all those who aided and consoled me, laboring with great fear in the visions that You have implanted in me from infancy, the reward of eternal light in celestial Jerusalem, so that through You they may rejoice in You without end." [*LDO Epilogus*]

The Natural History

The *Natural History* (also known as the *Book of Simple Medicine*) comprises nine parts. The first and longest covers more than two hundred plants, while subsequent books are devoted to the elements (including local German rivers), trees, precious stones, fish, birds, mammals, reptiles, and metals. Each is assessed for its utility to humans, either as food or as medicine. Often the description is limited to statements of the particular object's cardinal properties—the degree to which it is hot, dry, wet, or cold—as required for the version of humoral medicine that Hildegard professes. Unlike the three theological works, the medico-scientific writings are not presented in visionary form, but it may be that some kind of visionary preamble has been lost, as the manuscript tradition of these particular works is confused. They also differ from Hildegard's other works in containing a number of German words, especially for plants, fish, and some diseases. (The extracts are cited from the *Patrologia Latina*.)

FROM THE BOOK OF PLANTS

Spelt

Spelt is the best of grains. It is hot, rich, and full of goodness. It is sweeter than other grains. Eating it promotes sound flesh and healthy blood as well as a happy mind and joyful outlook. And however it is eaten, whether in bread or other food, it is good and pleasant. And if anyone is ill and cannot eat because of their infirmity, take the whole grain of the spelt and cook it in water, adding fat or the yolk of an egg so it will taste better and be more readily accepted, and give it to the sick person to eat and it will heal them internally, like a good and healthy poultice. [*Physica*, Plants, 5]

Hemp

Hemp is hot, and it grows where the air is neither very hot nor very cold, and that is its nature. Its seed is healthful and good for healthy people to eat. It is light and useful for the stomach because it lessens its accumulations and can be quite easily digested, reducing the bad humors and strengthening the good. But if those who suffer from headaches and light-headedness eat hemp, they will probably have a very minor headache. But it will not harm those who are quite well in the head and not light-headed. It will cause stomach pains for a while in those who are very ill, but it will not hurt those who are moderately ill to eat it. [*Physica*, Plants, 11]

Fennel

Fennel has a mild heat, and its nature is neither dry nor cold. Eaten raw, it will not harm a person. And however it is eaten it makes people glad, giving them a mild glow and a pleasant smell, and makes for good digestion. Its seed is also hot by nature and good for a person's health if it is added to other plants in medicines. For whoever eats fennel or its seeds daily on an empty stomach will lessen the bad and putrid humors and eliminate bad breath and make the eyes see clearly. [*Physica*, Plants, 66]

Yarrow

Yarrow is moderately hot and dry and has particular and subtle powers over wounds. For if someone is wounded by a blow, after the wound has been washed in wine cook the yarrow in a little water and when some of the water has been squeezed out, bind it lightly, still warm, over the cloth that is placed on the wound. In this way it will draw the pus and foulness and heal the wound. And let this be done as often as necessary, but when the wound begins to dry up and heal, then remove the cloth and without it place the yarrow directly on the wound and it will be more readily and perfectly healed. [*Physica*, Plants, 113]

FROM THE BOOK OF ELEMENTS

The River Nahe

The River Nahe arises from unclean waters originating in the sea from which certain clear streams sometimes flow. And therefore its course is very unpredictable, since it flows now swiftly and now sluggishly. And since it is rapidly checked and stops abruptly in its course, it does not have very high banks or shores. And it makes the skin white and thick, though wrinkled, and it does not harm the stomach, since its swiftness and sluggishness are not harmful, although it is unstable. Its fish are fat and good and do not go bad quickly. And its water is unpredictable, in that it runs now fast, now slow, but it does not disturb the bottom and so its fish are quite firm, since they find a plentiful supply of food in the river. [*Physica*, Elements, 9]

The Glan

The Glan has its origin in other streams, and so its water is rather sharp but healthy, being good for food and drink and baths and for washing the face. Its fish are healthy but do not keep a long time, on account of the sharpness of the water. Its sand is beautiful and clean. [*Physica*, Elements, 10]

FROM THE BOOK OF TREES

Bay Tree

The bay tree is hot and a little dry and signifies constancy. So take the bark and leaves of the bay tree and pound them and express their juice, and with the juice and triticale flour make little cakes, and reduce them to powder. Then with water and honey make a drink and put a little of the powder in and drink it, or take the powder and drink it in wine, and do this as often as you like, and the stomach will be cleansed of all impurities and not much harmed.

And cook the roots and bark and leaves of this tree in water, and make an ointment from this with goat's fat, and if you have a pain in the head or in the chest or in the side, back, or kidneys, rub the place with it and you will feel better. And the fruit of this tree is very hot and a bit dry and useful for medicine. If you often eat it raw it will reduce all fevers. [*Physica*, Trees, 15]

Broom

Broom is very hot. So let those suffering from leprosy squeeze broom in their hands to express the juice and smear it on themselves often, so assuaging and lightening their affliction.

Alternatively they can cook its flowers up in butter to make an ointment and apply it frequently to themselves, and the sores will diminish. And let those whose eyes are weak and dim gaze for a long time on the flowers of the broom, until they become moist and watery. They can also place the flowers on their eyes when they go to sleep and if they do it often their eyes will become clear. . . . [*Physica*, Trees, 50]

FROM THE BOOK OF PRECIOUS STONES

Emerald

The emerald is formed early in the morning, at sunrise, when the sun is positioned powerfully in its circle ready for its journey. Then the fresh greenness of the earth and crops is at its strongest, since the air is still cold and the sun already hot; and then the plants suck up the green freshness like a lamb sucking milk, since the heat of the day is scarcely sufficient to dry up the greenness of the day and nourish the things that are fertile to produce fruit.

And so the emerald is strong against all human debility and weakness, since the sun conditions it and all its matter is from the fresh greenness of the air. So let whoever has a pain in the heart or stomach or side have an emerald with them so they can warm the flesh of their body with it, and they will be better. But if those diseases overwhelm them so that they cannot escape their storm, then let the person place an emerald in the mouth and wet it with saliva, and thus as the saliva is made warm by the stone repeatedly being put in and taken out, the recurrent waves of the illness will surely cease.

And if anyone suffers from epilepsy and falls to the ground, place the emerald in their mouth and their spirit will revive, and after they get up and take the stone from their mouth let them look at it carefully and say: "Just as the spirit of the Lord filled the globe of the earth, so let it fill the home of my body by His grace so that it can never be moved," and let them do this for nine consecutive days in the morning, and they will be cured.... [*Physica*, Stones, 1]

FROM THE BOOK OF FISH

The Sturgeon

The sturgeon is of the hot rather than cold air and loves the nocturnal splendor of the moon and stars, preferring night to day. It rests during the day, and its delight and strength is in strongly flowing currents of water, and by the effort of swimming in them it makes its flesh soft. And it swims in the middle of the water and rarely goes to the bottom. Since it feeds on clean food, its flesh is good for healthy people to eat, though it harms the sick somewhat. And it spawns like other fish.

Let the person in whom dropsy has begun to worsen put the bladder of this fish in water, so that the water takes on the taste of it, and drink often of it, and the dropsy will get better and vanish. For the bladder of this fish is watery and harsh and rather bitter, and so when it is tempered by the sweetness of the water it diminishes the disease. [*Physica*, Fish, 2]

FROM THE BOOK OF BIRDS

The Ostrich

The ostrich is very hot, since its nature is like that of animals. It has wings like a bird but does not fly with them, since it runs very fast like an animal and lives on the ground and crops the fields. And it is so hot that its eggs would burn and its chicks not hatch if it brooded them itself. And for that reason it hides them in the sand, where they are incubated by the dampness and heat. But after the chicks come out of the eggs they follow and run with the mother as other birds do.

A person suffering from epilepsy should often eat the flesh of the ostrich, since it will make them strong and lift the frenzy of the disease from them. The flesh is healthy to eat for those people who are fat and vigorous, since it will diminish their superfluous flesh and make them strong; but it is not good for the thin or weak, being too rich for them. And the melancholic person who is heavy and slow in mind should eat it often and the melancholy will lessen, making the mind pleasant and cheerful by lightening it. The heart and lungs and inner organs of the ostrich are not good for medicine, because it does not really have the virtues of either bird or beast. [*Physica*, Birds, 2]

The Nightingale

The nightingale is hot and rather dry. It gets its life from nocturnal airs and is wholesome. And since this is so, it delights and sings in the night rather than in the day, since the sun shines too brightly for it in the day and it dislikes that.

And let those whose eyesight is dim catch a nightingale before the break of day and take its gallbladder and empty it and to it add one drop of dew found on clean grass, and then often anoint the eyelids and lashes that are around the eye, on retiring to bed—and if it touches the eye inside a little it does no harm—and the dimness will be marvelously removed from the eyes. [*Physica*, Birds, 49]

The Glowworm

The glowworm is more cold than hot. If someone suffers from epilepsy, when they have fallen down, let living glow-worms be tied in a cloth, as many as can be had, and placed on the stomach, and the person will immediately be revived. [*Physica*, Birds, 70]

FROM THE BOOK OF ANIMALS

The Unicorn

The unicorn is more hot than cold, but its courage is greater than its heat, and it eats clean plants and prances as it goes, and flees humans and other animals except those of its own kind and so cannot be caught. And it greatly fears and shuns men; just as the serpent in the first Fall shunned man and looked to woman, so this animal turns from men and follows after women.

There was a certain wise man who studied the ways of animals and wondered greatly that this animal could not be caught by any arts. One day he went hunting as he often did, and men and women and girls went with him. The girls went away from the others and played among the flowers. And a unicorn, seeing the girls, stopped its prancing and went a little way, and then some distance from them sat down on its haunches and looked searchingly at them.

And the wise man, seeing this, thought very hard about it and understood that the unicorn could be caught by girls, and coming on him from behind he caught him by means of those girls. For the unicorn, seeing a girl from afar, marvels that she has no beard, in spite of having the form of men; and if there are two or three girls at the same time, he wonders more and is more readily captured while he feasts his eyes on them. The girls by which unicorns arc caught must be noble and not peasants, not wholly grown up, or too little, but in mid-adolescence. Those are the ones he loves, because they are sweet and kind.

And regularly, once a year, the unicorn goes to the land that has the milk of paradise, where he seeks out the finest plants and digs them up with his hoof and eats them. And he gets much strength from these and so is able to flee all other animals. . . .

Take the liver of a unicorn and grind it up and add the powder to fat prepared from the yolk of an egg and so make an ointment. There is no form of skin disease that if often smeared with this ointment will not be cured, unless the patient dies or God does not wish to cure it. [*Physica*, Animals, 5]

The Dog

The dog is very hot and has a natural affinity for the ways of people, and so he knows and understands them and loves them, and willingly lives with them and is faithful. There-

fore the Devil hates and abhors dogs, because of the faithful-
ness they show to people. And the dog recognizes hatred
and anger and perfidy in a person and often growls at such a
one; and if he knows there is anger and hatred in a dwelling,
he will grumble and growl to himself in that place. And if
any man has treachery in him, the dog will bare his teeth at
him, although the man loves the dog; he growls because he
senses and understands this in the man.

And if there is a thief in the house, or anyone who has
the intention of stealing, the dog will snarl and growl at him
and behave differently toward him than to others and follow
after him and sniff at him with his nose, and in his way the
thief will be known. And he senses a little beforehand those
deeds and events, happy or sad, that are going to happen,
and gives voice according to his understanding and indicates
them: when they are going to be happy he wags his tail
gladly; when they are going to be sad he howls mournfully.

The heat that is in a dog's tongue confers health on
wounds and ulcers, if he touches it with this heat. But if
shoes are made from dog skin it makes the feet painful from
the uncleanness that it contains, being often saturated with
unclean sweat from its flesh.

And its flesh is of no use to people. Indeed, its liver and
innards are poisonous and its breath is noxious. And if a dog
chews on any bread or other food or if it drinks from any
drink, a person should not eat or drink what is left, because
while the dog can enjoy the food or drink, since he infects
these remains with poison, if a person afterward eats or
drinks them, then they take in the poison themselves.

The dog has soft flesh, and its brain is not strong and it
is often touched by evil clouds. And from time to time the
dog itself smells watery and putrid vapors in which airy spir-

its perform their tricks and wicked suggestions, and at such times he growls. And the rest of his parts are not much good for medicine. [*Physica*, Animals, 20]

The Mole

The mole is cold and likes to live in rich, muddy soil, and it avoids the poor soil, casting aside what is inferior and bad and useless and remaining in that which is good and salubrious. And it cannot see, because it does not live above ground, but it has a great internal knowledge and smells and understands where to go, and it eats earth. And its flesh is no good for people to eat because it is nourished by dampness, nor is it good for any medicine. [*Physica*, Animals, 37]

The Mouse

The mouse is hot and has devious ways, ever fleeing; and for that reason its flesh is contrary to man's and it is not much good for medicine. But if a person has the falling sickness and falls to the ground, and afterward gets up, put a mouse in a little pot and give the water to the person to drink, and wash their forehead and feet with the water, and let it be done as often as they fall down and they will be cured. For since a mouse flees everything it will also flee the falling sickness.

And when a mouse is going to give birth and suffering pain and difficulty, it goes in distress to a riverbank and there seeks very tiny stones and takes as many as it can hold in its mouth, then runs to its nest and spits them out and blows on them. Then it sits on them and warms them and then immediately gives birth; but after delivery it spurns them and kicks them away and then sits on its young and warms them. And if someone finds these stones within a month of their being thrown away and then ties them on the stomach of a pregnant woman who is in labor but cannot give birth, she soon will, and after she has been delivered they should immediately be thrown away. . . . [*Physica*, Animals, 39]

FROM THE BOOK OF REPTILES

The Viper

The viper is as hot as fire, and all that is in it is deadly and it will not let anything live near it that it can overcome. It is so malicious that vipers flee from other vipers until it is time for them to mate. In the region where vipers live, if any man finds a dead viper, since he will not catch a living one, let him make a great fire from strong wood in a secret place where there are no people and throw the dead viper on the fire and then quickly withdraw from that place, lest its venom or bad vapors touch him. After it has been reduced to ashes, if there is anything left of it, leave that aside and take its ashes and the ashes of the coals in which it was burned and put them by in a linen cloth. And then if anyone has a swelling, let them put this cloth with its ashes on the swelling, and it will immediately subside. [*Physica*, Reptiles, 11]

The Earthworm

The earthworm is very hot and grows in that green freshness where seeds begin to germinate, and increases in the vibrancy of this greenness and because of its clean nature has no bones, and like other useful things such as cinnamon, is good and beneficial. For the earth has a certain dampness in it by which, as if by veins, it is held together so it does not crumble, and when rain is about to fall from the air this dampness in the earth feels the rain is about to come by which the veins of the earth will be filled, and the earthworm, understanding this by its nature, comes out on account of the filling of the vessels of the earth.

If a person has scrofula, at the time when the earthworms surface because of the falling rain let him catch enough of them and put them in a pot or jar and smoke them a bit with barley straw so that they die. Then add spelt flour and stir them hard with an oaken stick, and then a little wine and an equal measure of vinegar, and mix them again as if making a paste. Put this paste on the boils before they burst, for three days, and the cleanness of the clean worms will diminish the uncleanness of the flesh. . . . [*Physica*, Reptiles, 17]

FROM THE BOOK OF METALS

Gold

Gold is hot, and its nature is partly like the sun and partly like the air. Let anyone who is paralyzed take gold and heat it so there are no impurities in it and beat it to a powder and take a little flour—about a handful—and knead it with water and add about an obolus of gold powder to this. Let this be eaten fasting in the morning, and again on the second day make a cake with flour and the same weight of gold, and let it be eaten fasting. And a cake prepared in this way and eaten will keep the infirmity in check within a year.

And let the gold lie on the stomach for two months, and it will not make it worse or ulcerate it, and if it is cold and slimy it will warm and purge it without danger to the person. Now if this is done to a healthy person it will keep them healthy, and if they are sick it will make them well.

And again take pure gold and place it in a pot or jug, and when it is heated put it in pure wine so that it is warmed by it, and let the patient drink it warm. And let it be done often, and the illness will depart.

And if anyone has a fever in the stomach, let them warm pure wine with the heated gold and thus drink it, and the fever will leave them. And if a tumor appears in any part of the body, let them warm the gold in the sun and draw it around the edge of the swelling, and the tumor will disappear. And let a deaf person make a poultice with powdered gold and flour as described above and put a little in the ears, so that its heat is transferred to the ears. And if it is done often they will regain their hearing. [*Physica*, Metals, 1]

Brass

Brass is hot and is made from something else—like limestone from stone—since brass is not of its own nature but made from another metal, like a knight who is not a knight by his own birth but is made a knight. Therefore it is not good for medicine but rather harms than heals. So if a person were to put a brass ring on their finger, or if they were to warm any other part of their body with it, they would attract greater infirmity than health to themselves. [*Physica*, Metals, 6]

Causes and Cures

This book, also known as the *Book of Compound Medicine*, begins with an account of cosmology and cosmography and proceeds to an outline of the place of mankind in the world. This is followed by a précis of the basis of humoral medicine, which includes some striking departures from the tradition and a short description of more than two hundred diseases and conditions that afflict mankind. Remedies for some of these illnesses (mostly herbal, as foreshadowed in the *Natural History*) follow. The rest of the work proceeds according to no discernible pattern, and includes chapters on uroscopy, cherries, and a series of astrological prognostications based on the phase of the moon at the time of conception (*lunaria*). (For ease of identification, pending the appearance of a critical edition, the extracts are cited according to the Copenhagen manuscript numbering by book and chapter and the page number of Kaiser's edition.)

ABOUT HAIL, SNOW, AND RAIN

Hail is like the thunder's eye. But when the sun is in decline in winter it does not transmit its fire to the heavenly heights, burning under the earth rather than above it. Therefore it cannot flame in the heavens. So the waters that are in the upper regions become like powder shaken from the cold and send out snow. But when afterward they are more gently heated, they send rain. And when from time to

103

time the sun displays moderate heat, not too hot and not too cold, then it sends a gentle rain, in the same way that humans, from time to time when they are happy, quite often shed tears of joy. [C&C, 1.10; K4]

ABOUT THE FIRMAMENT AND THE WINDS

The firmament contains fire, the sun, the moon, the stars, and the winds. It is constituted by means of all these things, whose qualities make it firm so that it does not fall apart. For as the soul maintains the entire human body, the winds hold together the entire firmament so that it is not brought down. And they are invisible, just as the soul is invisible, coming from the mystery of God. And just as a building will not stand without its cornerstones, so neither the earth nor the abyss nor the entire globe and all that goes with them can exist without these winds, because all such things are ordered and maintained by them.

For the earth would completely disintegrate and fall asunder if it did not have these winds, just like a body if it had no bones. The chief eastern wind sustains the entire eastern part, the chief western wind, the western part, the chief southern wind, the southern part, and the chief northern wind, the northern part. [C&C, 1.13; K5]

ABOUT THE QUALITIES OF THE EARTH

The earth is cold by nature and has seven qualities. Namely, that it is cold in summer and hot in winter; that it contains green freshness and dryness; that it produces shoots and sustains animals, and that it carries all things. So God worked for six days and rested on the seventh, when He subjected to Man's use all the things that He had made.

Now in summer the earth is cold beneath the surface, since the sun by the strength of its rays is productive. In winter, however, it is warm beneath the surface, otherwise it would be fragmented by the cold dryness. And thus it shows fresh greenness in its heat, and in its cold, dryness. For in winter the sun is not fruitful above the ground and concentrates its heat beneath the earth, so that the ground can preserve various seeds, and so it puts forth all shoots by means of heat and cold.

And it bears up the animals that run and move upon it, so that they are not bogged down, as it is hardened by the cold and the heat and can thus support all things firmly. And God so placed the earth that it might bring forth shoots at the appropriate time, and at the appropriate time be wanting in shoots, just as the moon waxes and wanes. [*C&C* 1.47; K30]

About the Various Results of Conception

Now when a man in the emission of his strong seed and in proper kindly love for a woman goes to her and the woman also bears a proper love for the man at the same time, a male child is conceived, since thus it is ordained by God. For it cannot be otherwise than that a male child will be conceived, for Adam was formed from clay, which is a stronger material than flesh. And the male will be prudent and virtuous, since he was conceived in strong seed and in the proper kindly love which they both had for each other.

If, however, this love is lacking in the woman toward the man, but the man has in that hour proper kindly love for the woman, though not the woman for the man, and if the seed of the man is strong, a male will still be conceived, because the kindly love of the man will prevail. But this male will be weak and not virtuous since here the love of the woman for the man was deficient.

And if the man's seed is thin, but he loves the woman and she has the same love for him, then a virtuous female will be created. But if the man loves the woman but the woman does not love the man, or if the woman loves the man and he does not love her and the man's seed is thin at that time, then a female will be born on account of the weakness of the seed.

But if the man's seed is strong, but neither the man nor the woman feel love for the other, a male will be conceived, because the seed was strong, but it will be bitter from the bitterness of the parents. But if the seed is thin and neither feels kindly love toward the other at the time, a female will be born of bitter temperament.

The heat of a woman who is fat by nature will overcome the seed of the man, and so the infant will often take after her in appearance. But women who are thin by nature often produce a baby who features the father. [*C&C* 2.8; K35–36]

THAT THE FOUR ELEMENTS ARE
PRESENT IN HUMANS

Now the Elements, that is, fire, air, earth, and water, are present in humans, and they work in them with their powers and in this working they quickly turn about like a wheel in its revolutions. For fire with its five powers is in the human brain and marrow, since when Man was first changed from clay the shining fire burned in his blood out of God's fortitude, and so blood is red. And the fire's heat is shown in human sight, chill in smelling, moisture in taste, airiness in hearing, and motion in touch.

But air, with its four qualities already mentioned, is in human breath and reason. For by the living breath, which is the soul, it ministers to those who bear it and it takes wing, where they draw breath in and exhale it, so they can live. And the soul is fire that permeates the whole body and makes mortals live. Air also kindles fire, and fire burns in all things by means of air. Air stands for the dew in emission; fresh greenness in excitation; breath in motion; and heat in the human's moving about.

But water, with its fifteen powers, which have already been mentioned, is in the humors and blood. [*C&C* 2.27; K 43]

ABOUT THE FLOOD

When Adam was expelled from Paradise, the water before the Flood was not so swift in its passage nor so fluid as it afterward was. But it was as if it had a kind of covering over it that held it back somewhat and so it flowed little by little. And the earth was not clayey but dry and friable, since it was not yet perfused by the water. And from the first edict it gave forth fruit above measure.

Then humanity forgot God and followed the ways of beasts rather than the ways of God. So many preferred beasts to humans and mingled and consorted with them, both women and men, so that the image of God was almost obliterated in them. And the whole human race was transformed and transmuted into monsters, so that some people even conducted themselves like beasts, in both their behavior and utterances—in running and howling and manner of life.

For the beasts and animals before the Flood were not yet as fierce as they afterward became. They did not flee people, nor did people flee them, nor were they terrified of each other. And the animals and beasts willingly dwelt with the people, and they with them, because they had in the beginning almost the same origins. But animals and beasts intermingled with people and people with them, whence they loved each other greatly and unwontedly and were bound to each other. Yet Adam fathered certain sons who were filled with divine reason because they wished to practice no wickedness. And because they remained in holiness, they were called the sons of God. [*C&C* 2.37; K 47–48]

MANKIND AND THE ELEMENTS

Now as mentioned above, in the same way that the Elements comprise the world, so too are they the fabric of the human body. And they are diffused and active throughout the body so that the body is held together, and at the same time they are spread throughout the world and work upon it. For fire, air, water, and earth are in human beings, and human beings are made from them.

Thus from fire they derive heat; from air, breath; from water, blood; and from earth, flesh. Moreover, their sight comes from fire; their hearing from air; their movement from water; and their measured tread from earth. And the world prospers when the elements fulfill their roles in a well-ordered fashion, so that heat, dew, and rain, one by one and in moderation, apportion themselves in due season and come down to regulate the earth, bringing fruitful and abundant produce and health. But if they were to fall on the earth suddenly, all at once and unseasonably, the earth would cleave asunder and its produce and health would be ruined.

Likewise, when the elements are properly at work in the body they preserve it and confer health; but when they are at odds in it they weaken and kill it. For the humors, coagulated from heat, moisture, blood, and flesh in the human body, when they penetrate and remain in it and work there peacefully and in due proportion, are healthy. If, on the other hand, they reach it all at once, rushing upon it too copiously, they will weaken and destroy it. For heat and moisture and blood and flesh have all been changed, because of Adam's sin, into antagonistic humors in mankind. [*C&C* 2.42; K 49–50]

ABOUT A WOMAN'S DESIRE

Desire in a woman can be compared to the sun, which gently and lightly and carefully perfuses the earth with its heat so that it can yield fruits, because if it were to burn more fiercely in its constant care, it would harm the fruit rather than foster it. So desire in a woman is gentle and light but constant in its heat so she can conceive and bear a child, for if she were always in a fever of desire she would not be suitable to conceive and give birth. And when desire arises in a woman, it is lighter than a man's since such fire burns less strongly in her than in him. [*C&C* 2.95; K 76]

DREAMS

Since the human soul is from God, sometimes when the body is sleeping people see true things that are to come, and learn of things that have not yet occurred but that sometimes do. But it often happens that their mind is disturbed or stirred up by a devilish illusion, and they cannot with certainty see or understand such things. For it is frequently the case that people who are weighed down by the thoughts and opinions and wishes that occupied them while awake can be made light by their acting like the yeast which makes a mass of flour rise, whether these thoughts are good or bad. [*C&C* 2.110; K 82–83]

MIGRAINE

Now migraine arises from black bile and from all the evil humors that are in a person. And it afflicts half the head and not all of it, so that sometimes it is on the right side and sometimes the left. That is, when the humors are in excess it affects the right side, but when black bile prevails, the left. Now migraine is so intense that if it affected the entire head a person could not stand it. And it is difficult to get rid of because when, on occasion, the black bile lessens, then the bad humors increase, and when the bad humors are quiet it makes the black bile increase. This makes a cure hard, since black bile and bad humors are not easily calmed at the same time. [*C&C* 2.123; K 90]

OTHER KINDS OF HEADACHES

Food that has flowing juices in it, like the juice of garden plants and of apples, taken often without dry food such as bread sometimes produces headaches in people, but they are easily relieved since they arise from light juices. But phlegm is often excessive in humans, and it rises and goes to the head and presses the veins of the temples that sustain the forehead, making it painful. [*C&C* 2.124; K 90–91]

ABOUT THE STOMACH AND DIGESTION

The stomach is placed in the body so that it can receive and digest all food. It is retentive and a little rough on the inside so it can retain the food for digestion, and so that it does not slip away too soon, as a mason roughens the stone to hold and retain the mortar lest it slip away and fall.

But if a person takes in certain foods beyond measure, that is raw and uncooked or partly cooked food, or food that is too fatty or heavy, or dry and arid, then the heart and liver and lungs and other heat sources in the body cannot provide the amount of heat required by the stomach to process the food. Then they are coagulated and dry out and become moldy in the stomach, so that they cause either green or grey or pale or diverse humors in it. And they send evil humors and bad smells throughout the whole body like a putrid dung-pit and like green and damp wood, which gives out foul smoke when it is burned.

When certain foods are taken in, certain infirmities arise, since if there is too much undisciplined heat in the person the food will be burned up; or if there is too much cold, the food eaten will not be digested but coagulated and curdled, and thus it will remain in the person, causing illness. [C&C 2.153; K 99]

A HEALTHY DIET

Whoever wishes to be healthy should eat food that is cold by nature after that which is hot by nature; and take naturally hot food after that which is naturally cold. Food that is dry by nature should be eaten after food that is moist by nature; after food that is moist, food that is by nature dry should be taken. This applies whether the food is cooked or raw, and whether it is hot or cold by nature, so that the qualities can thus be tempered by their opposites. [C&C 2.222; K 136]

ABOUT THE CREATION OF ADAM AND EVE'S FORMATION

When God created Adam, Adam felt great love in the sleep that God sent to him. And God gave form to the love of the man, and thus the woman is the man's love. And soon after the woman had been formed God gave the man that power of creation so that by his love, which is woman, he could engender children. For when Adam looked on Eve he was filled with wisdom, for he looked on the mother through whom his children should be born.

And when Eve looked on Adam it was as if she was looking at Heaven or as the soul reaches upward yearning for heavenly things, since her hope was in the man. And so there is and should be only one love between a man and a woman and no other.

But the love of the man compared to a woman's is in its heat like the fire of burning mountains, which is difficult to put out—compared to a fire of wood which is easily extinguished. And the love of the woman compared to the love of the man is like the gentle heat of the sun which produces fruit, compared to a fiercely blazing fire of wood, since she gently offers her fruit in offspring. But the great love that was in Adam, when Eve was taken from him, and the sweetness of that slumber in which he was sleeping were turned to a contrary mode of sweetness by his transgression. And thus, since a man feels and possesses this great sweetness in himself, he runs swiftly to the woman as a hart to the fountain, and the woman to him, and she is like a threshing floor, which is flailed with many strokes and brought to heat when the grain is threshed upon it. [*C&C* 2.223; K136–7]

CONCERNING VARIOUS BEVERAGES

If land that is rich in grain produces wine, this is more healthful to the sick than wine produced from fruit-bearing land, that is to say, land that produces a moderate amount of grain, although it is more costly. For wine heals and makes people happy with its beneficial heat and great powers.

Beer puts flesh on the bones and gives a lovely color to

the face, on account of the strength and good juices of the grain. Water has a weakening effect and for the sick sometimes produces bad humors in the lungs, since water is weak and has no qualities of strength. But if one is healthy and drinks water in moderation it will do no harm. [*C&C* 2.255–6; K 150]

GOUT

Those who have soft and permeable flesh and who indulge in strong wine to excess are often struck by the disease called gout. Since their flesh is soft from too many drinks, the bad humors that are in them suddenly collect in one of their members and upset it like a fiery dart and like sudden great floods that knock down the mill and the buildings around it. And so these humors disturb the members on which they fall, unless prevented by the grace of God or the vital spirit that is in the person. But sometimes they do destroy a limb and even make it dead and useless. [*C&C* 2.279; K 161–2]

FALLING HAIR

When a young man first notices falling hair, let him take bear grease and a little ash made of wheaten or triticale straw and mix them together and smear his whole head with it, especially at the roots of the hair. Afterward he should not wash the ointment off. And the hair that has not yet fallen is thus moistened and made strong, so that it will not fall out for a long time. And let him do it often and refrain from washing his hair. For the heat of the bear grease is of such a kind that it will produce plentiful hair, and the ash of wheaten and triticale straw will strengthen it so it does not soon fall out. And when these work together, as described, the man's hair will be retained for a long time and not fall. [*C&C* 3.1; K 165–6]

MIGRAINE

Let the person who suffers from migraine take aloe and twice the quantity of myrrh and reduce it to fine powder and then take a similar amount of flour and add poppy seed oil to it. Make it into a poultice, and with this cover the whole head from the ears to the neck, with a cap placed over it, and wear it like this for three nights and days. For the heat of the aloe and the dryness of the myrrh, with the smoothness of the flour, tempered by the coldness of the poppy seed oil, will soothe the pain in the head, and a poultice made in this way restores the richness to the brain. [*C&C* 3.4; K 166–7]

A METHOD FOR STRENGTHENING THE TEETH

Whoever wishes to have healthy and firm teeth should, in the morning on rising from bed, take fresh cold water in the mouth and hold it there for some time. In this way the film that is around the teeth is softened. And wash the teeth with the water that is in the mouth, and do it often, and the film that is around the teeth will not increase and they will remain healthy. [*C&C* 3.19; K 173–4]

CURES FOR INSOMNIA

If a person is busied with certain problems and cannot sleep, if it is summer, let them take fennel and twice as much yarrow, cook them in a little water, and, having removed the water, let them put the herbs on the temples and forehead and tie a cloth over it. And take green sage and sprinkle it with a little wine and put it over the heart and around the neck and they will be rewarded with sleep.

But if it is winter take some fennel seed and yarrow root, cook them in water and place them around the temples and head as said before, and place powdered sage moistened with a little wine over the heart and around the neck, tied down with a cloth over the top, as described, and they will have better sleep. For the heat of the fennel induces sleep, and the heat of the yarrow makes it sound, and the heat of the sage slows the heart and dilates the veins in the neck, so that sleep may come.

And these herbs, excited to heat by the smoothness of warm water, are put around the temples so they can press upon the veins, and placed on the head and the forehead so that they will quieten the brain. But the fennel seed and yarrow are cooked in water because of the mildness of the water, and the powdered sage placed in wine so that a remedy may be produced from it. [*C&C* 3.37; K 184]

FOR A DIFFICULT BIRTH

And if a pregnant woman is struggling mightily to give birth, then with fear and great skill let gentle herbs like fennel and ground-ivy be boiled in water and strained. Let them be placed on her thighs and back and let them be tied there gently with a linen cloth, so that her pain and closure will be more gently and easily relieved. For the cold and bad humors that are in women sometimes block and close up a pregnant woman, but if the gentle heat of the fennel and the gentle heat of the ground-ivy are excited to fire in the gentle heat of the water and thus placed around her thighs and back—since these are the places she suffers most constriction—they will induce her womb to open. [*C&C* 4.3; K 188]

Concerning Immoderate Laughter

Let the person who is greatly affected and struck by immoderate laughter grind up a nutmeg and add half as much sugar and put it in warmed wine and drink it when fasting or having eaten. For immoderate laughter dries the lungs and harms the liver, but the heat of the nutmeg will heal the liver and the heat and juice of the sugar will restore the lungs. And since these things are tempered by the wine that has had its heat altered, thus applied they will restore the good humors destroyed by immoderate laughter. [*C&C* 4.22; K 199]

Steam Baths

For those who are thin and dry, a steam bath heated with hot rocks does no good, because they will be made more dry by it. But for those who have fat flesh, a steam bath is good and useful, since the humors that are superfluous in them are controlled and lessened. And baths with hot rocks are good for the lame because the humors that often rise up in them are somewhat assuaged in them by a steam bath. . . . [*C&C* 5.27; K 233–4

FROM THE *LUNARIA*

Prognostications for the Nineteenth Day

Whoever is conceived on the nineteenth day of the moon, if male, will be simple and not cunning but agreeable to people, and he will lack pride in things unless he is helped by others, and he will be healthy in body, but he will not live for a long time. And if a female, she will be stupid, yet amiable to others, and in her pride she will easily fail unless she is supported by others. And that woman will easily fall ill and soon recover, but she will not have a long life. [*C&C* 5.52; K 239]

The Symphonia

The origin of Hildegard's cycle of more than seventy liturgical songs—hymns, sequences, antiphons, versicles, and responsaries—the full title for which seems to have been the *Symphony of the Harmony of Celestial Revelations*, lies in the compositions Hildegard wrote for the communal worship of her own establishments, especially after the move to Rupertsberg. Later, it seems, she provided pieces for other monasteries, such as those celebrating St. Disibod for Disibodenberg and for the monasteries of Trier pieces treating their patron saints, such as St. Matthias and Eucharius.

The place of the *Play of the Virtues*, a short version of which appears (without music) as the last vision in the *Scivias*, is problematical, since it is also included in some manuscripts of the *Symphonia*. This remarkable musical drama depicts the plight of an errant soul wavering between the blandishments of a choir of virtues and the Devil. It may have been performed by the nuns at the dedication of the church on the Rupertsberg in 1152. (The songs are cited according to item number in Newman's edition; the *Play of the Virtues* comes from Dronke's edition.)

ANTIPHON FOR THE DIVINE WISDOM

O power of Wisdom
ringing the circuit,
comprehending all
in one vital path.

Of your three wings
one flies to Heaven
the second sweats from Earth
the third flies everywhere.
Praise be to you, as is fitting
O Wisdom.
[*O virtus Sapientiae*, Newman 2]

ANTIPHON FOR THE CREATOR

Oh, how wonderful is
the prescience of the divine Heart
who foreknew all Creation.
For looking on the face of Man new-formed,
He saw completed in this form—Creation.
Oh, how wonderful is the breath
that breathed Man to life.
[*O quam mirabilis*, Newman 3]

ANTIPHON FOR THE REDEEMER

O shed blood
that rang on high
when all the elements
clashed together
voicing their woe
and trembling
as the blood of their Creator
touched them,
salve our sickness.
[*O cruor sanguinis*, Newman 5]

HYMN TO THE HOLY GHOST

O fiery spirit, praise be to You
who work in timbrels and lutes!

The minds of men take fire from You
and the tabernacles of their souls contain their strength.

Whence will ascends and imparts a taste to the soul
and his light is desire.
Understanding calls to You with sweetest sound,
and prepares buildings for You with Reason distilling golden
     deeds.

You always hold the sword to sever
what the poisoned apple brought through blackest murder
when will and desire are clouded
and the soul flaps and circles.
But the mind is the bridle
of will and desire.

Now when the spirit raises itself as it seeks
to see the pupil of evil and jawbone of wickedness
You swiftly burn it in fire
when You wish.

But when Reason through ill deeds lies prone
You strain and beat upon it with force
and restore it by the infusion of experience.

When evil draws a sword against You,
You strike it to the heart
just as You did with the first fallen angel
when You cast the tower of his pride into Hell.

And there You raised another tower
of publicans and sinners
who confess their sins and deeds to You.

Whence all creatures
receiving life from You, praise You,
for You are the treasured ointment
for broken and stinking wounds
when You convert them into treasured gems.

Now deign to gather us to You
and guide us to proper paths. Amen.
[*O ignee spiritus, laus tibi sit*, Newman 27]

ANTIPHON FOR THE VIRGIN

The closed gate today
has opened for us
what the serpent stifled in the Woman.
So in the dawn shines
the bloom of the Virgin Mary.
[*Hodie aperuit nobis*, Newman 11]

ANTIPHON FOR THE VIRGIN

O leafy branch,
standing nobly
in the coming dawn:
now be glad and rejoice
and deign to free our frailty
from evil ways
and reach out your hand
to raise us up.
[*O frondens virga*, Newman 15]

ANTIPHON FOR THE VIRGIN

O most splendid jewel,
clear beauty of the sun,
which was poured into you,
a fountain leaping
from the Father's heart,
that is the peerless Word
through which He created
the world's first matter
overturned by Eve.

For you the Father fashioned
this Word as man,
and so you are that clear material
through which this very Word exhaled
all virtues
as He led forth from primal matter
all creatures.
[*O splendidissima gemma*, Newman 10]

ANTIPHON FOR THE VIRGIN

Oh, what a great miracle it is
that into a subject female form
the King entered.
God did this
because humility rises above all.
And oh, how great is the happiness
in this form
because malice,
having flowed from Woman,
a woman later washed away
and gathered all the sweetly smelling virtues
and adorned Heaven
more than she had disordered Earth.
[*O quam magnum miraculum est*, Newman 16]

SONG TO THE VIRGIN

Hail, O greenest branch
who came forth in the gusty breath
of the questions of the saints.

When the time came
for you to branch into flower,
"Hail Mary" was proclaimed
because the heat of the sun worked in you
like the odor of balsam.

For in you flowered a comely bloom
who gave savor to
all the spices
that had been dry.
And they all appeared
in their full freshness.

Whence the heavens dropped dew on the grass
and all the earth was glad
since her womb brought forth wheat
and the birds of the air
built their nests in it.

Then a banquet was made for mankind
with joy for all the feasters.
Whence, O sweet Virgin,
there is no end of joys in you.
But Eve despised all these things.
Now let there be praise to the Highest.
[*O viridissima virga*, Newman 19]

SEQUENCE FOR THE VIRGIN

O rod and diadem of royal purple,
you are like a breastplate unbroached.
Your branching flowered in contradiction
to the way Adam brought forth all mankind.

Hail! Hail! From your womb
a different life came forth
from the life that Adam denied his sons.

O flower, you were not budded by the dew
nor drops of rain, nor the circumambient air,
but Divine Light brought you out
from this most noble stem.

O stem, your flowering
God foresaw on the first day of His creation.

And with His Word made you the golden matter,
O Virgin worthy of praise.

Oh, great is the strength of man's side,
from which God took the form of woman,
and made her the mirror of all adornment,
the clasp of His entire creation.

Then the celestial harmony sounded
and all Earth marveled,
O praiseworthy Mary,
because God loved you so.

Oh, how lamentable and dismal it is
that sorrows and wrongs at the serpent's word
flowed into Woman.

For that woman, whom God placed as mother of all,
ruined her womb with wounds of ignorance
and brought great sorrow on her children.

Yet, O Dawn, from your womb
a new Sun came forth, to wipe out all Eve's sin
and through you brought a greater blessing
to humankind than all Eve's hurt.

Whence, O saving Lady, who brought
new light to all mankind
unite the members of your Son
in celestial harmony.
[*O virga ac diadema*, Newman 20]

ANTIPHON FOR ST. BONIFACE

St. Boniface, an eighth-century missionary to Germany from England, was known to Hildegard as the first archbishop of Mainz and a martyr for the faith in Frisia (now Holland).

O Boniface
the Living Light saw in you
the likeness of a wise man
who returned to their source
the pure streams flowing from God
when you watered the greenness of the flowers.
So in your friendship for the living God
you are a crystal shining
in the benevolence of righteous ways
where you ran wisely.
[*O Bonifaci*, Newman 51]

RESPONSORY FOR ST. DISIBOD

Hildegard is the principal source of information about St. Disibod. Indeed, all we know about him comes from the *Life* she wrote at the request of Abbot Helenger. In it he is pictured as a seventh-century bishop, exiled from his native Ireland, who after much wandering built a hermitage on Disibodenberg and founded the first monastery there.

O happy soul
to trample down
your earthborn body,
an exile from the world.
So you are crowned
by divine Reason
and made its mirror.

And the Holy Spirit
considered you
its habitation.
So you are crowned
by divine Reason
and made its mirror.
[*O felix anima*, Newman 43]

SEQUENCE FOR ST. URSULA

The story of St. Ursula was a particular favorite of Hildegard's.
In it, Ursula, a British princess, seeking to avoid marriage to a
pagan prince, made a pilgrimage to Rome together with eleven
thousand maiden companions and on the way back was massa-
cred by the Huns outside Cologne.

O Ecclesia
your eyes are like sapphire
and your ears like the Mount of Bethel
your nose is like a mountain of myrrh and incense
and your mouth like the sound
of many waters.

In a true vision of faith
Ursula loved the Son of God
and turned away from her husband and this world
and gazed on the sun
and called to the most beauteous youth
saying:

With great longing
have I desired to come to you
and abide with you in celestial marriage,
running to you by a strange path
like the clouds which fly in pure air
like sapphire.

And after Ursula had spoken thus,
news of it spread among the people.
And they said:
In girlish ignorance the child
knows not what she is saying.

And they began to mock at her
with great music
until the fiery burden
fell upon her.

Then they all understood
for rejection of the world
is like the Mount of Bethel.

Then the Devil
entered his minions
and they killed
the most noble lives
in those bodies.

And this, with a loud cry
all the Elements heard
and before the Throne of God
they said:

Woe! the red blood of the innocent Lamb
has streamed out
in its coupling.

Let all the heavens hear this.
And with highest music
praise the Lamb of God!
As the throat of the ancient serpent
with these pearls
of the substance of God's word
has been choked.
[*O Ecclesia*, Newman 64]

ANTIPHONS FOR ST. URSULA

The ardor of divinity
gave the kiss of peace 'mid high applause
to the virgin Ursula
and her flock
before all the people.

Wherever they went
they were feted,
a foretaste of Paradise,
deserving high honor
for their godly way of life.

From their native land
and from other regions
wise monks joined with them
to guard their virginity
and serve them in all things.

For God himself
foreshadowed in the first woman
that in man's guardianship
a woman should be nurtured.

For the air flies,
doing its duty by all Creation,
sustained by the firmament,
nurtured by its strengths.

And so these girls
were sustained by the greatest man
bearing the standard of the kingly Child,
born of the Virgin.

For God sent dew on them
and their fame multiplied
so that all the people
fed on their fame as if it were bread.

But the Devil in his envy
laughed it to scorn
and left untouched
no work of God.
[*Studium divinitatis*, Newman 63]

ANTIPHON FOR ST. JOHN THE EVANGELIST

O mirror of the dove
of form undefiled,
who gazed on the mystical gifts
in the purest fountain;

O wondrous flowering
that never faded and fell
sent by the most high Gardener.

O most sweet repose
of the embrace of the sun:
you are the special son of the Lamb
in chosen friendship
of the new lineage.
[*O speculum columbe*, Newman 35]

SEQUENCE FOR ST. DISIBOD

O bishop of the true city,
who in the temple of the cornerstone
reaching toward Heaven
bowed down on earth
for God.

A pilgrim from the seed of the world,
you longed to be an exile
for the love of Christ.

O mount of secret thought,
your care was to show a beautiful face
in the mirror of the dove.

You hid yourself from sight
drunk with the smell of flowers
shining before God
in the windows of the saints.

O shaft of the keys of Heaven
since you exchanged the world
for unclouded life,
this prize, sweet witness,
is ever yours in the Lord.

For in your mind
the living fountain spouting light
leads forth streams of purity
by the way of salvation.

You are a great tower
before the altar of the highest God
veiling the summit of this tower
with clouds of spices.

O Disibod, through your light
and the agency of pure sound
you have raised aisles of wondrous praise
on two sides through the Son of Man.

You stand on high,
unashamed before the living God
and you protect with vivifying dew
those praising God with these words:

Oh, sweet the life
and holy the determination
which in our blessed Disibod
ever built the glorious light
in heavenly Jerusalem.

Now let there be praise to God
from those who wear the goodly tonsure
striving manfully.

And let the citizens of Heaven rejoice
in those who follow their example.
[*O presul vere civitatis*, Newman 45]

SEQUENCE FOR ST. RUPERT

Hildegard also wrote the *Life of St. Rupert*, the patron saint of
her own convent. In it Rupert's difficult early days as the son
of a devout Christian mother and pagan father are described.
After the father dies, Rupert and his mother are able to devote
themselves to godly and charitable pursuits until his death at
the age of twenty. His mother Bertha founded a monastery
that was sacked by the Normans in the ninth century, but
which Hildegard was able to revive by her move there in 1150.

O Jerusalem, golden city,
adorned with kingly purple,
O building of highest goodness,
a light never darkened.
You are graced
with the dawn and the heat of the sun.

O blessed boyhood
shining in the dawn
and O praiseworthy youth
flaming in the sun.
For you, O noble Rupert, gleamed gemlike
whence you cannot be hidden by fools
just as the valley cannot hide the mountain.

Your windows, Jerusalem,
with topaz and sapphire are mightily adorned.
You shine in them, O Rupert, and cannot be hidden
by those of little faith—
like the valley and the mountain,
crowned with roses, lilies and purple
in a true showing.

O tender flower of the meadow
and O sweet sap of the apple
and O harvest without pith,
which does not divert hearts to sin.
O noble vessel, which is not defiled
or consumed in the dance
of the ancient cave—not oozing
with wounds of the ancient destroyer.

In you the holy Spirit makes music
while you stand among the angelic chorus
shining in the Son of God
since you have no stain.

What a seemly vessel you are, O Rupert,
who in your childhood and youth,
God-fearing, sighed for God
in the embrace of love
and the sweetest odor of good works.

O Jerusalem, your foundation is laid
with scorching stones,
that is, with publicans and sinners
who were the lost sheep—
but found by the Son of God
they ran to you and were placed in you.

Then your walls flash
with living stones,
which by greatest efforts of goodwill
have flown like clouds in Heaven.

And so your towers, O Jerusalem
glow and blaze in the dawn
and heat of the saints
and through all the ornaments of God,
which you do not lack, O Jerusalem.

Whence you, O decorated
and O crowned ones

who dwell in Jerusalem
and you, O Rupert,
who are their fellow in that dwelling
help us, your servants, laboring in exile.
[*O Ierusalem, aurea civitas*, Newman 49]

SEQUENCE FOR ST. EUCHARIUS

Eucharius, the first bishop of Trier, lived in the late third century. Medieval legend has it that he was one of the seventy-two disciples of Christ and that he subsequently came to evangelize Gaul.

O Eucharius
you walked in the joyful path
when you dwelt with the Son of God,
touching Him
and seeing the miracles he wrought.

Him you loved completely
when your companions were sore afraid
because they were but men
not fully able
to comprehend the good.

But you embraced Him
in burning love of perfect charity
when you gathered to yourself
the harvest of His commands.

O Eucharius,
you were much blessed
when the word of God
tried you in the fire of the dove
when you were made to shine like the dawn
and so fashioned the foundation of the Church.

And in your breast
the day shines forth
in which three shrines
stand on a marble pillar
in the City of God.

Through your mouth the Church savors
the old and the new wine
which is the draught of holiness.

And in your teaching
the Church reached understanding
so that she proclaimed upon the mountains
that the hills and woods should bow down
and take suck from her.

Now in your clear voice
beseech the Son of God for this crowd
lest they fail in God's rites
but ever prove a living sacrifice
before the altar of God.
[*O Euchari*, Newman 53]

SEQUENCE FOR ST. MAXIMIN

Maximin was a fourth-century bishop of Trier and patron saint
of another of the monasteries of Trier with which Hildegard
corresponded. The sequence is concerned to celebrate priest-
hood in general rather than Maximin's particular life or legend.

The dove looked in
through the window grates
where before his face
balm was crystallizing
from shining Maximin.

The heat of the sun blazed
and shone in the darkness

whence a gem budded
in the building of the temple
of the purest loving heart.

He, the highest tower
of the tree of Lebanon
and cypress made,
has been adorned with jacinth and sardonyx,
a city outshining the skill of any builders.

He, the swift hart, ran
to the fount of purest water
flowing from the mightiest stone
which runs over with sweet perfumes.

O perfumers
enjoying the sweetest greenness
of the king's gardens,
mounting on high
when the holy sacrifices
have been fulfilled with the rams,

Among you shines this architect,
the wall of the temple
who desired the wings of the eagle
kissing his nurse Wisdom
in the glorious fecundity of the Church.

O Maximin,
you are the mountain and the valley,
and an edifice in both
where the goat walked with the elephant
and Wisdom knew delight.

You are strong
and gentle
in the glittering rites of the altar,
mounting up like the smoke of incense
to the column of praise,

Where you intercede for the people
who reach toward the mirror of light
for which there is praise on high.
[*Columba aspexit*, Newman 54]

VIRGIN'S SONG

O sweetest Lover!
O sweetest Enfolder!
help us to guard
our virginity.

We were born in dust
alas, alas, and in Adam's crime.

It is very hard to resist
what tastes of the apple.
Set us upright, Savior, Christ.

Our burning desire is to follow You.
Oh, how heavy it is
for such wretches
to follow the pure and innocent
King of Angels.

Yet we trust in You
and Your desire
to seek a gem in the dust.

Now we call on You, Husband and Consoler,
who redeemed us on the cross.
We are joined to You in a marriage of your blood,
rejecting men
and choosing You, Son of God.

O most beautiful Form!
O most sweet savor of desirable delight!
We ever sigh after You

in fearful exile;
when will we see You and dwell with You?

We are in the world
and You in our minds
and we embrace You in our hearts,
as if we had You here.

You, the prepotent Lion, broke through the heavens,
descending into the chamber of the Virgin,
and overcame death,
building life in the Golden City.

Grant us citizenship in it
and to remain in You, O most sweet Spouse,
who has wrested us from the jaws of the Devil,
who ruined our first parent.
[*O dulcissime amator*, Newman 57]

THE PLAY OF THE VIRTUES

FROM THE PROLOGUE AND SCENE 1

Patriarchs and prophets:
Who are they, who are like clouds?

Virtues:
O saints of old, why do you marvel at us?
The Word of God shines forth in human form
and we shine with Him,
building up the members of His beautiful body.

Patriarchs and prophets:
We are the roots and you the branches,
the apple of the living eye,
and we were in its shadow.

Complaint of the embodied souls:
Oh, we are pilgrims.
What have we done, turning to sin?
We should be daughters of the King,
but we have fallen into the shadow of sins.
O living Sun, carry us on your shoulders
to the most just inheritance that we lost in Adam!
O King of Kings, we fight in your battles.

....

Unhappy soul:
Oh, I know not what to do
or where to flee!
Oh, woe is me, I cannot perfect
the garment I wear.
Indeed, I wish to throw it off!

Virtues:
O unhappy conscience,
O miserable Soul,
why do you hide your face from your Creator?

Knowledge of God:
You do not know or see or understand Him who made you.

The soul:
God created the world:
I do Him no harm
but I wish to use it!

The Devil, shouting to the soul:
What is the point of your working foolishly, foolishly!
Look to the world and it will embrace you honorably.

....

From Scene 3

Virtues:
Alas, alas, we Virtues lament and weep,
because the Lord's sheep flees life!

Lament of the penitent soul invoking the Virtues:
O you regal Virtues, how beautiful
and how shining you are in the highest Sun,
and how sweet is your dwelling—
and so, oh, woe is me, because I fled from you!

Virtues:
O fugitive, come, come to us, and God will take you up.

From Scene 4

Chastity:
In the mind of the highest, O Satan,
I placed my heel on your head,
and I nurtured a sweet miracle in virgin form,
when the Son of God came into the world.
So you are cast down with all your spoils,
and now let all the inhabitants of Heaven rejoice,
because your belly has been confounded.

Devil:
You know not what you nurture, because your womb is empty
of the beautiful form assumed from man—where you transgress
the injunction which God gave in sweet copulation; so you
know not what you are!

Chastity:
What have your words to do with me,
since they pollute with wicked filth?
I produced one Man, who through His birth
gathered to Himself the human race
in your despite.

Saints' Lives

These examples of narrative writing show a further aspect of Hildegard's style. The *Life of St. Rupert* may have been written as early as the 1150s to provide a focus for the new foundation at Rupertsberg. The *Life of St. Disibod* was written some twenty years later, at the request of Abbot Helenger, during the period that Hildegard was writing the *Book of Divine Works*. It should be noted that Hildegard is the only authority for the lives of these particular saints, although she may have been drawing on local and monastic traditions, especially in the case of St. Disibod. (Citations are by numbered paragraph from *Patrologia Latina*.)

FROM THE LIFE OF ST. RUPERT

Rupert's Infancy and Boyhood; A Prophetic Dream; The Building of the Hospital

Now the blessed Rupert, when he was a babe at the breast, did not display the fretful behavior of infancy as in crying and tantrums; and when he was weaned he spent his childhood like one who longed for God with most diligent intent. And so his father hated him and many times while he lived declared that he was stupid and simple. But those who worshiped God in true and good faith, seeing that the lad was so kindly disposed in his childhood, loved him dearly and said truly that he would have a blessed future, although in ignorance. For the Holy Spirit, which had suffused the patriarch Jacob in his mother's womb, also inspired this child, because God very often performs His miracles in those who because of the softness of their marrow and veins have not attained full knowledge. . . .

And when he reached the age of twelve, his mother said to him: "My son, since we have much property and wealth, let us make an oratory in honor of God and for the salvation of our souls." To which he replied: "No, my mother, first let us see what the Bible says." And the prophet said: "Deal your bread to the hungry, and bring the needy and the harborless into thy house." And again: "When thou shalt see one naked, cover him, and despise not thine own flesh" (*Is.* 58:7). His mother, hearing this, was exceedingly joyful because her son had given her such sound counsel.

For through the Holy Spirit, good and holy desire welled up like balsam in the mind of this youth, and he silently considered how the things which had been said might be done, and so he fell asleep. Then, through the intervention of the Holy Spirit, he saw in his dream an old man with a beautiful face who washed little boys in clear water, and afterward took them to an orchard—lovely with every kind of flower and trees and full of the odor of all sorts of perfumes—and dressed them in the whitest of garments.

And the blessed Rupert, drawn to the beauty of the place, said to the old man: "I wish to stay here." To which the old man replied: "You cannot remain here now, since you will prepare a fruitful ladder for yourself into Heaven, where you will be a companion of the angels. So do not neglect to carry out what you have decided about the poor, since through feeding and clothing them, you will eat the bread of life and put on the clothes that Adam lost through disobedience, and, being made an exile from the world and in your mind, you may choose for yourself the better part."

And when the blessed boy Rupert awoke he told his mother the things that he had seen in his sleep. At this she rejoiced greatly, and, bowing her knee to God, she prayed, saying, "O my Lord God, you will fulfill my heart's desire in my son." And then the mother and son together built certain dwellings next to the river of flowing waters, where they cared for the poor and the naked, to whom they gave food and clothing with the help of faithful and holy men. One of these was called Wigbert, who served them as priest; and the other, who acted as their assistant, was unlettered. And the blessed Rupert himself, forgetting his tender age and nobility for the love of God, many times washed the feet of the poor, served them food and drink, and very often made their beds. And thus he faithfully served the Lord until his fifteenth year. . . . [*Rupert*, 4–5]

Rupert's Final Illness and Death

And in his illness, the old man whom he had previously seen in his sleep appeared to him, saying: "I am the Ancient of Days, who appeared to Daniel in a nocturnal vision; and now I show myself to you and call you to the glory of eternal blessedness, since by the orchard which I showed you in a vision before, I truly predicted the good and holy deeds that you have now completed." And Rupert, when he awakened from his sleep, overcome by sadness and fear because he well understood that he had freely completed what he had vowed to God in his longing, told his mother what he had seen. And she, immediately struck by overwhelming sorrow, gave voice to such groans and lamentations as can be imagined by anyone similarly afflicted. And when this blessed one had suffered for thirty days in the illness, God took him from this life in the twentieth year of his age, well-shriven and God-fearing, lest if he had reached full maturity he might have fallen into the ways of his father, because He who knows all predetermined thus to set him free. So God prevented this and withdrew him from the present life shining in innocence. . . . [*Rupert*, 10]

Rupert's Burial and Miracles; Bertha's Subsequent Life and Death

In the oratory, then, which he and his mother had constructed on their property above the Rhine, he was buried with a great assemblage of people from the entire region. Some wept over him because he was taken from the present life so young; others rejoiced because, by a miracle which God worked through him, the whole of the region was illuminated, as the day by the sun.

And for eight years God performed many signs and wonders through the merits of His beloved in that place, in the sick, the lame, and in prisoners; so that anyone beset by tribulation coming to his tomb might be liberated by the grace of God.

But the blessed Bertha, God's chosen widow, after the happy death of her son, led a holy life in great contrition of heart from that time on. And she offered all the things that she received at her son's tomb for the service of God. And she gave freely from such things all that was needed for the congregation of brothers who there served God in matters divine. Thus after the death of her son, she lived for almost twenty-five years in great goodness, with fasting, almsgiving, and prayers, and she completed many works for the love of God piously and justly. Then, stricken by bodily infirmity, she gave back her spirit to God, whom she had always fixed upon in heavenly desire, and in peace was honorably buried on that estate, in the tomb of her son. [*Rupert*, 10–11]

FROM THE LIFE OF ST. DISIBOD

St. Disibod's Early Career in Ireland

. . . and so as he increased in virtues and in age, he was admitted to the grades of the sacred orders, reaching the priestly order at the age of thirty. And when he received it in the fear of God he acted like a good perfumer, who plants in his garden certain aromatic plants and spices, always taking care that the garden is green and not dry.

And the saint was mindful in these endeavors of the words of Wisdom, where it says: "I have gathered my myrrh with my aromatical spices" (*Cant.* 5:1). Which is to be understood thus: I, who should exert myself in works of justice, with good application show to God the mortification of my flesh, since I have become for love of Him an exile from vices, and I desire to flee their common wickedness and have no fellowship with them, since I hasten to love and worship that true God in the odors of the virtues. Thus with the love of celestial desire coming from my heart, and with His help, it will not fail.

And the saint in this righteous and holy will was as if dead to the world, so that many seeing these things acted as if they did not know him and shrank from his company, because he obliged himself completely to serve the spirit rather than the flesh.

And when he had served God with these virtues in praiseworthy manner and on account of this was blameless and pleasing to those who love God, it happened that the bishop of those parts crossed over from the present to the future life; and when the people, great and small, convened as was the custom, to choose another bishop for themselves, some of them who knew the upright and honest life of the blessed Disibod unanimously elected him to be their bishop. But some of them whose way of life was reprehensible vetoed the action, saying, "What is the good of making a silent and unspeaking man master, who does not know the people?" [*Disibod*, 5–7]

His Difficulties as Bishop

And when the blessed man was forced to assume the burden by the more prudent, he, protesting he was unworthy of such a great honor, drew back his hands and feet with all his strength; but at last, impelled and overcome by those who feared God, although unwilling, he was by divine ordination placed on the episcopal throne. In which office the fortunate bishop began to declare and teach the justice of God, and he warned all he could to subject themselves to God, and what he had been filled with from his infancy by the Holy Spirit he now showed forth in teaching and proved by good examples of holiness and virtue with paternal affection to them. Some, because of the merits of the virtues that they saw in him, loved him and were eager for his teaching and opened the ears of their heart, but others, who had cast God behind them, cried out in frenzy against the saint: "He lives as if he were not human and forces us to live inhumanly. And who can listen to him?" And they heaped many injuries on him. . . .

And when he had lived for many years without eradicating their evils and even sustained danger to his body, afflicted with weariness, he said in his prayers to God with great lamentation: "O God, and O judge of all the holy! What does it profit me to labor with these people who rend your justice with rabid bites?" And then the partisans of these errors, with the people implicated in the same, seeing that this blessed man would not consent to their errors and wickedness but everywhere constantly opposed them without fear of death, at last with the help of a troop of unbelievers expelled him—much put upon—from his see. [*Disibod*, 9, 12]

St. Disibod Leaves Ireland for Germany

But he, preferring to serve God in quietness rather than to tarry without the fruits of utility, with the few religious men he had collected to the seat of his dignity—which he had ruled firmly and religiously for ten years—left his native land and all he had for Christ's name, saying that it would not profit him or anyone else for him to remain there, where he had execrated such great unbelief together with the hardness of iniquity. So for the sake of eternal life he embarked upon the pilgrimage that he had so long desired with joyful soul.

And when he had left Ireland and traveled through many regions and inspected many places diligently, seeking repose for his soul, at last he came to Germany, where he found a hard and cruel people, and, exhausted, sought a halt for a while. And when he gave those people the words of salvation and examples of holiness, many, when they heard him, loved him—though many cared neither to hear nor to love him. . . . [*Disibod*, 12, 13]

St. Disibod Settles at Disibodenberg

Then the blessed Disibod was encouraged in the hope that his worthy desire would be fulfilled through the help of God, when he heard good report of the people living in the part of Gaul on this side of the Rhine—namely that though they were a hard people yet they maintained the faith of the Church, devout in their living. He grew tired of the jeering laughter of the people, and without delay made a journey to the Rhine region. Then diverging, and walking through certain byways, he reached the river Glan, and having crossed it he saw a high, wooded mountain, which he ascended after ten years of wandering, and there, worn out, he stopped and rested. And he said to his companions—there were three, the first and oldest being Gillilaldus, the second Clemens, and the third Salustus—who had come with him from Ireland, touched by the Holy Spirit: "Here will be my repose."

And when he had walked all around the mountain, and considered it from every side, its pleasantness as a place to live delighted his soul because its height would make access difficult to those who came, and the streams flowing on either side would give refreshment of body to those living there; and he prayed, saying: "O Lord who resides above the heavens and rules the abyss, I pray that the beauty of this place may be turned to the beauty of souls; because it is fitting that You be served in this place by a faithful people." And, so saying, he devised for himself a dwelling at the foot of the mountain, toward the east because of the convenience of the water, and, vigorously beginning the life that he had long desired with prayers and vigils and fasts, he lived a solitary existence of harshness and difficulty.

And the companions who had come with him, for their mutual convenience, in penitential mode constructed separately each his house at a distance from him. And it should be noted that they were sustained for quite some time there by the roots of plants, since they had no other food. . . . And it happened that when men from time to time came into the woods to hunt wild beasts, or to fish in the adjoining stream, or for firewood, or for other necessities, they would often see this holy man digging up roots or collecting other necessary things, and so after some time he was revealed.

So the rumor went out among the people that a certain holy man with some others had come to that place, sent by God. And many, wondering at this, came to him with goodwill, and they discussed with him certain things pertaining to themselves, and to them he replied with the words of salvation and life (since from the time of his exile to that time he had especially taken pains to learn the language of those people, so that he could understand and speak it). And so it was that those to whom he gave the words of life and warnings about eternal life would very often give to him and those staying with him things that were necessary for the body. So the servant of God and the men associated with him gathered to them the poor and needy, and with whatever remained to them above their daily needs they fed them. . . . [*Disibod*, 16–19]

Life at Disibodenberg

Many signs and miracles were performed through him in the blind and deaf and lame and in those possessed by the Devil and even in those who lost their senses in a tempest of evil humors, who were brought to him from far away and nearby. And they were all healed through him, since the power of God was in him.

For that servant of God lived among his people as a hermit, which is the living root of the monastic life, because those following this way of life, withdrawn from the world in all things, live in solitude with the praise of the angels. Such a life is so difficult that many cannot sustain it from frailty of body as much as mind, if they come to it imprudently and suddenly. The blessed father, living in this strict manner, prepared those under him for every good work, by teaching and example, like the man who makes a burning fire burn strongly, and they did not seek or want another leader while he was alive. . . . [*Disibod*, 29]

Final Illness and Death; Miracles at His Tomb

When the holy man of God had labored for a long time, and when the strength of his body had almost failed through excessive toil, he predicted in fearful spirit that they could not always remain in such prosperity and security as they had enjoyed to that time without adversity; but they would suffer many great pressures and tribulations, since the Devil, whom they had cast into much confusion by their good lives, strove mightily to overthrow them by the great scorn which he was exerting himself to produce among the people.

At length he consoled them much and piously, saying: "I have labored until now in sighs and sorrow of heart, greatly desirous that you do not suffer tribulation while I live in this world, though I believe in the Lord that it will come. But know that after my death, which will come swiftly (since the strength of my body is already gone), and after the tribulations that you will suffer, the latter times will be better and more prosperous. Indeed, you and those who come after you will be more abundantly supplied in all the needs of your bodies and souls than when I am alive."

And when they heard these things they lamented with great sorrow and tears, since they understood his end to be at hand. . . .

And he indicated the place of his burial to them, and he begged with tears and groans that they should bury him not in an exalted place but in the humble shelter of his oratory, where he had served God alone. And they promised they would do so, weeping with great sorrow. Also sorrowing, they enumerated all his good works and teachings one by one and with bitter tears cried out: "Alas, alas, what will become of us when we lose the guardian and consolation of our bodies and souls?" And as the thirsting hart seeks the fountains of waters, thus they desired to keep him longer. . . .

And then, when his illness grew worse, having again called the brothers, he indicated to them as far as he could that his end was near; and after much labor and after many tribulations, in the eighty-first year of his age, on the eighth day of July, he reached the end of his present life. And in their presence he gave back his soul to the Lord, whom he had faithfully served. And at his passing a most sweet smell like the odor of myrrh and incense and of balsam immediately ensued, and many signs appeared there.

News that the blessed Disibod had gone from this life immediately spread throughout the whole province, whence a great number of people, hastening to his obsequies, desired to be present at his burial and to see the signs that the Lord would perform there. And that most sweet smell which had appeared at his passing remained around his tomb until the thirtieth day after his death, during which time seven people obsessed by evil spirits, thirty lame, many blind and deaf, and very many others suffering from various other illnesses, on touching his tomb, were truly healed by the grace of God. [*Disibod*, 32–35]

Correspondence

Almost four hundred letters attributed to Hildegard have
been transmitted in various manuscripts from the Middle
Ages which display the writer under several aspects. In the
majority of them she adopts the role of God's mouthpiece,
relaying His warnings about failure of leadership to high eccle-
siastics and secular rulers and more direct advice about how
to deal with monastic and spiritual problems to those in the
religious life and the privileged laity. The letters vary greatly
in length, from several pages to a few lines. Sometimes the
letter is in the form of a sermon; often it is cast in visionary
form. Only rarely do we get a glimpse of Hildegard in her
human frailty, notably in the exchange of letters concerning
the nun Richardis of Stade. (The letters are cited from van
Acker by volume and letter number where possible, and otherwise by page from *Pitra*.)

LETTER TO BERNARD OF CLAIRVAUX
(CA. 1146–1147)

The Cistercian abbot Bernard of Clairvaux (1090–1153) was
one of the most influential religious forces in Europe. At the
time of this letter his former pupil Bernardo Pignatelli had
recently been elected pope Eugenius III and Bernard was
preaching the Second Crusade on his behalf with great suc-
cess. It was at his urging that the Pope read a portion of the
Scivias and approved Hildegard's writing at the Synod of Trier
in 1148.

O venerable Father Bernard, greatly honored in the power of God, you who are a terror to the lawless stupidity of this world, and who with burning love for the Son of God and great fervor wonderfully enlist men in the army of Christ under the banner of the holy cross for the worthy struggle against the ferocity of the pagans, I beg you, through the living God, that you listen to these, my questions.

Father, I am most troubled about this vision which appeared to me in the spirit of mystery, and which I never saw with the eyes of the flesh. I, wretched and more than wretched in that I bear the name of woman, have seen great miracles, which my tongue could not describe had not the spirit of God taught me that I may believe.

Most assured and gentle Father, reply in your goodness to me, your unworthy servant, for from my infancy I have never lived one hour free from care. In your piety and wisdom consult your soul as taught by the Holy Spirit, and grant heartfelt consolation to your handmaid.

For concerning texts, I know the inner meaning of the expositions of the Psalms and the Gospels and of the other volumes, which are shown to me in this vision. It touches my breast and mind like a burning flame and teaches me such profundities of exposition. But it does not give me literary expertise—this I do not have—in German, for I only know how to read simply, not how to analyze a text. I seek your response to this, because I am a person untaught from any external source, being taught inwardly in my soul. That is why I speak doubtfully.

But hearing from your wisdom and your piety I will be comforted, since I have not dared to say these things to anyone except a certain monk whom I have observed to be more upright than the rest, because there are many heresies abroad, as I have heard people say. And I have shown all my secrets to him, and he has indeed supported me, for these things are great and fearful.

I wish that you might console me, Father, for the love of God, and I will be certain. I saw you two years ago in a vision, like a man who does not fear to gaze upon the sun, completely undaunted. And I wept because I am so ashamed and fearful. Good and most mild Father, I have been placed in your charge, so you can reveal by these words whether you wish me to speak openly or hold silence, because I am sorely pressed in that vision to say what I have seen and heard. In it, meanwhile, I am laid on my bed by great infirmity because of my silence, and so I cannot raise myself.

Therefore I weep with sorrow before you, since I am fickle in my nature, with the motion of the winepress, the tree born of the root springing in Adam from the suggestion of the Devil, whence he became an exile in the pilgrimage of the world. Now rising, I run to you and say: You are not fickle, but ever hold the tree aloft. You are the victor in your soul, not raising yourself only, but the world to salvation. For you are an eagle gazing on the sun.

I entreat you, through the serenity of the Father and through His admirable Word, and through the sweet sap of compunction, the Spirit of Truth, and by the holy Sound through which all creation rings, and through that Word from whom the world sprang, and through the sublimity of the Father, who in sweet greenness sent the Word into the Virgin's womb, whence He assumed flesh as honey is surrounded by the honeycomb. And may that Sound, the power of the Father, fall upon your heart and rouse your soul that you do not become indifferent to the words of this person, as long as you seek all things from God, either for the person, or for that secret, until you cross through the threshold of your mind and know all these things in God. Farewell, farewell in your soul, and be strong in God's struggle. Amen. [v.A. 1.1]

TENGSWICH OF ANDERNACH
(1148–50 OR POSSIBLY AS LATE AS 1170)

This letter is a response to one sent by Tengswich, the head of a house of canonesses at Andernach. In it, under the guise of politely and humbly seeking instruction, she expresses her amazement at certain practices rumored to occur in Hildegard's convent. These include the wearing of elaborate festal costumes by the nuns, with silk veils and crowns, and the fact that Hildegard will only admit those of the highest nobility to her establishment. The inclusion of Hildegard's answer among her collected letters indicates that her contemporaries believed that all such criticism had been effectively trounced.

The Living Fountain says: "Let a woman hide herself in her chamber and preserve her modesty, because the serpent breathed great perils of horrible lust into the first woman. How? The form of woman shone and sparkled in the primal root, and in her was formed the part in which every creature lies hidden. How is this? In two ways, first, by being made by the finger of God, and then, because of her exalted beauty. Oh, what a wonderful being you are, founded in the sun and conquering the earth!

"But the apostle Paul, who flew in the heights and was silent on earth, so that he did not reveal what was hidden, observed this: The woman who is subject to the male power of her husband, joined to him through the primal rib, should have great modesty, so that she does not give or reveal her own vessel, which belongs to her husband, in another place that is not appropriate for her. And let her do this according to the word that the Lord of the Earth declares in the Devil's despite: 'What God hath joined together, let no man put asunder' (*Mt.* 19:6).

"Now hear: The earth sweats forth fresh greenness in the grass, until winter overtakes it; and winter carries away the beauty of its flowering, and covers the freshness of its flower so that it cannot reveal itself, as if it had never dried up, because winter spirits it away. So a woman should not exalt herself in her hair nor adorn it, nor crown it with any diadem or gold ornament, unless at the desire of her husband, according to his pleasure and then in moderation.

"This does not apply to the virgin; she stands in the simplicity and beautiful integrity of Paradise, which will never appear dry but ever remains in the full greenness of the flowering branch. The virgin is not directed to cover the freshness of her hair, but she covers it from her own will in greatest humility, since a person will hide the beauty of the soul lest the hawk carries it off through pride. Virgins are joined in the Holy Spirit to the pure dawn of virginity: whence it is only right that they come to the highest priest, like an offering dedicated to God. Wherefore it is fitting that by license and by the revelation of the mystical breath of the finger of God, a virgin may be dressed in a white garment in clear reference to her marriage to Christ, seeing that the mind is made one with the interwoven whole, considering who it is to whom she is married, as it is written: 'They have his name and the name of his Father, written on their foreheads' (*Ap*. 14:1). And again 'These follow the Lamb whithersoever he goeth' (*Ap*. 14:4).

"For it is God who keeps watch over every person so that the lesser order does not rise above the higher, as did Satan and the first man, who wished to fly higher than their positions allowed. Now what man would collect all his stock in one barn—oxen, asses, sheep, and kids—and prevent them scattering? And so separation is needed in this case, lest diverse people gathered in one flock be scattered in the pride of their elevation or in the ignominy of their difference, and especially lest proper behavior should break down there, as they rend each other with hatred as the higher order falls on the lower and when the lower gains ascendancy over the higher. For God distinguishes the people on earth as in Heaven, as angels, archangels, thrones, dominions, cherubim, and seraphim. And they are all loved by God, but are not of equal repute. Pride loves princes and nobles for their elevated station but hates them when they do away with it. And again it is written, 'God doth not cast away the mighty, whereas he himself also is mighty' (*Jb*. 36:5). He Himself is not a lover of persons, but loves the works which derive their taste from Him, just as the Son of God says: 'My meat is to do the will of my Father' (*Jn*. 4:34). Where humility is, there Christ always prepares a feast, and so it is necessary that those who love vain honor better than humility are identified, when it seems that such things are preferable. The diseased sheep is cast out lest the whole flock be contaminated.

"God imbued people with good understanding, so that their name might not perish. For it is good that people do not seize a mountain that cannot be moved, but stay in the valley, little by little learning what they can understand.

These things are said by the Living Light and not by any person. Let them who hear, see and understand whence they come." [v.A. 1.52R]

RICHARDIS OF STADE (1151–1152)

Richardis of Stade joined Hildegard at Disibodenberg and moved with her to Rupertsberg. She is mentioned in the prologue to the *Scivias* as one of the people who helped Hildegard with its writing. The situation with which the next three letters are concerned is described in one of the autobiographical sections of Hildegard's *Vita* written by the monks Godfrey and Theodorich: "While I was writing the book *Scivias* I held a certain noble girl . . . in great affection, just as Paul loved Timothy. She allied herself to me in diligent friendship in everything and consoled me in all my trials until I completed the book. But after this, because of her noble connections, she turned aside to the honor of a higher position and was elected head of an important foundation [Bassum, in the diocese of Bremen]. . . . Soon afterward she left me, and in another place, far away from me, she gave up the present life and the dignity of her appointment." (*Vita*, bk. 2)

Hear me, O daughter, your mother talking to you in the spirit: My sorrow rises up, my grief is destroying the great faith and consolation I had in a human being. Henceforth let me say: It is better to trust in the Lord than to put confidence in princes. That is: A person should look to the life above without any shadowing of love and lessening of faith, which the airy humor of the earth renders transitory. A person thus looking to God fixes his eye like an eagle on the sun. And for this reason one should not pay attention to a high personage who withers as the flower falls. I erred thus for love of a noble person.

Now I say to you: As many times as I sinned in this way, God showed that sin to me either through certain pains or through sorrows, just as has now happened with you, as you well know.

Now again I say: Alas for me, mother, alas for me, daughter, why have you abandoned me like an orphan? I loved the nobility of your behavior, your wisdom and chastity, your soul and your entire life, so that many said: What are you doing?

Now let all those have a sorrow like my sorrow, who had in the love of God such love in their hearts and minds for a person—as I had for you—who was seized in a moment from them—just as you were taken from me—weep with me. But may the angel of God go before you and the Son of God protect you, and may His mother keep you safe. Remember your sorrowing mother Hildegard, that your happiness fail not. [v.A. 1.64]

LETTER TO HARTWIG OF BREMEN (1151–52)

Hartwig was Richardis's brother. In this letter Hildegard seems to lay the blame principally at the door of Cuno, abbot of Disibodenberg. Richardis's mother, the marchioness of Stade, had been helpful to Hildegard in securing the site of Rupertsberg, as had Hermann of Stahleck, Count of the Rhine Palatinate.

O person worthy of praise, having the things necessary for one who is in succession to the highest God, that is the office of bishop, so may your eye see God, and your sense understand His justice, and your heart burn in God's love, that your spirit fail not. But stand with highest zeal building the towers of Heavenly Jerusalem, and God will give you as helper that sweetest mother—Mercy. And be a bright star shining in the darkness of the night of depraved men, a swift hart running to the fountain of living water. See how in this time many pastors are blind and lame, robbers of the wages of death, smothering the justice of God.

O dear one, your soul is greatly pleasing to me because of your family. Now hear me, prostrate at your feet with bitter tears, for my soul is mightily sad, since a certain horrible man has cast aside my advice and desire—and that of the rest of my nuns and friends—concerning our most dear daughter Richardis, dragging her from our cloister through his unbridled will. Since God, who knows all things, knows where pastoral care is useful, the faithful person should not go about seeking office. And if such people go around restlessly seeking mastery, desiring the pleasure of power rather than consulting the will of God, they are like ravening wolves, and their souls never faithfully seek spiritual things. That way lies simony.

Whence there was no necessity for our abbot to preempt the holy soul in the blindness of his senses and his ignorance of these matters and the great rashness of his unseeing mind. If our daughter had remained quietly, God would have readied her for His own glorious will.

Therefore I implore you who sit on the episcopal throne in the order of Melchisidech, asking you through Him who gave His life for you and through His most noble Mother, that you send my most beloved daughter to me—for I do not neglect the choice of God or contradict it wherever it might be—so that God may give you the blessing that Isaac gave to his son Jacob, and bless you with the benediction that He gave through His angel to Abraham for his obedience.

Now hear me, not casting aside my words as your mother and sister and Count Hermann cast them aside. I would not do you injury without its being for the will of God and the salvation of your sister's soul, but I ask that I may be consoled by her and she by me. I do not gainsay what God has ordained.

May God give you the blessing of the dew of Heaven, and may all the choirs of angels bless you, if you hear me, the servant of God, and if you fulfill the will of God in this matter. [v.A. 1.12]

TO THE SAME (CA. 1152)

Oh, how miraculous is the salvation of those souls which God so gazed upon, that His glory in them is not overshadowed. For God works in them like a strong fighter who takes care that he will not be overcome by anyone, but that his victory may be secure.

Now hear, O dear one. So it was in the case of my daughter Richardis, whom I call both my daughter and my mother, for my soul was full of love for her since the Living Light taught me to love her in a most powerful vision.

Hear, then. God held her in such high regard that the pleasure of the world could not embrace her; but she always fought against it, although she appeared like a flower in beauty and grace and in the harmony of this world. But when she was yet among us I heard this said of her in a true vision: "O virginity, you stand in the king's bedchamber." For she had fellowship in the virginal branch and the most sacred order, whence the daughters of Sion rejoice. But the serpent of old wished to withdraw her from that blessed honor, using the nobility of her worldly position. But the highest Judge drew this, my daughter, to Himself, cutting all human glory from her. Whence my soul has great faith in her, although the world loved her beautiful appearance and her wisdom, while she lived in it. But God loved her more, and so did not wish to give His love to a rival lover—the world.

Now dear Hartwig, sitting in Christ's place, fulfill the will of your sister's soul, as obedience demands. And as she was always solicitous for you, so you must now be for her soul, and perform good deeds according to her desires. Whence I too shall cast that sadness from my heart, which you have caused me on account of my daughter. May God grant you, through the prayers of the saints, the dew of His grace and a blessed reward in the life to come. [v.A. 1.13R]

TO ELISABETH OF SCHÖNAU (CA. 1152–56)

Elisabeth was a somewhat younger contemporary of Hildegard's who entered the Benedictine community at Schönau in about 1140. Her visionary career took some time to develop, and initially her apocalyptic prophecy was not as well received as Hildegard's writing. However, her visions authenticating recently discovered relics such as those of St. Ursula and the eleven thousand virgins became immensely popular.

I, a poor little woman—a fragile vessel—say these things not from myself but from the Serene Light: "Man is a vessel that God fashioned for Himself and that He filled with His inspiration, so He may perfect His works in him. For God does not work as humankind does, but so that all things may be perfected according to the commands of His precepts. The plants, forests, and trees appeared, the sun also, the moon and stars came forth to support them, and the waters produced fish, and birds, cattle, and beasts arose, which all serve mankind as appointed by God.

"Man alone did not know Him. For when God gave Man great knowledge, in his mind he exalted himself and turned from God. For God had looked on Man that He might perfect all His works in him, but the old deceiver played him false and infected him with the crime of disobedience with the delight of an ill wind, when he sought more than he should.

"Ach, oh woe! Then all the Elements folded in on themselves in the variations of light and darkness, just as Man did in transgressing the precepts of God. But God succored certain men, lest humanity be totally mocked. For Abel was a good man, but Cain was a murderer. And many saw the mysteries of God in the light, but others committed many crimes until that time came when the Word of God was made clear, as was said: 'Thou art beautiful above the sons of men' (*Ps.* 44:3). Then the Sun of Justice came forth and illuminated men with good deeds in faith and in work, just as the dawn comes first and the rest of the hours of the day follow until nightfall. Thus, O daughter Elisabeth, the world is changed. For now the world has run through the time for cultivating its virtues, that is to say the dawn, the first, the third, and that vital sixth hour of the day. But in this time it is necessary for God to succor other people, lest such instruments be useless.

"Hear, O anxious daughter, that the ambitious suggestion of the ancient serpent sometimes fatigues the people who are thus filled with the inspiration of God. For when that serpent sees a beautiful gem, he writhes, saying: 'What is this?' And he harasses such people with many miseries as the afflicted mind desires to fly above the clouds, like gods, just as he himself did.

"Now hear again: Those who wish to perform the works of God should always remember that being human they are fragile vessels, and always observe what they are and what they will be, and leave heavenly things to Him who is heavenly. For they are exiles, not knowing heavenly things, but singing the mysteries of God as a trumpet which of itself gives no sound, nor works except when another breathes into it that it may sound. But they should put on the breastplate of faith, being mild, meek, poor, and wretched, just like the Lamb whose trumpet's sound they are. And they should be as innocent children, since God always chastises those who play on His trumpet, foreseeing that their fragile vessel will not perish, but be pleasing to Him."

O daughter, may God make you the mirror of life. But I who am downcast in my wavering mind and greatly troubled with cares and fears, from time to time sound like a small blast of the trumpet from the Living Light; and so may God help me to remain in His service. [v.A. 2.201R]

HILDEGARD TO POPE EUGENIUS (1153)

A letter of general admonition with the somewhat obscured agenda of defending Henry, archbishop of Mainz from 1142 to 1153, when he was deposed by the papal legates Bernard of St. Clement and Gregory of St. Angeli.

The Living Eye sees and says: "Who knows and discerns

every creature, and who raises them all up, watches. The valleys cry out against the mountains, and the mountains fall on the valleys. How is this? The subordinates are stripped bare of the discipline of the fear of God, and so they are incensed madly to ascend the mountain peaks, and find fault with the prelates. And their rashness does not accuse their wicked deeds. But they say: 'I am useful and should be made a prelate for my usefulness.' And they hold all the works of prelates unworthy, because they reject the notion that they are better than themselves. So the subordinates are black clouds and their loins are not girded, but they scatter all the seeds of the field, saying that these things are worthless. And they do this because they are poisonous with envy.

"The poor man is very foolish, since his vestments are torn, and he always looks at the colorful garments of others but does not wash his own from filth. For the mountains skip over the key of the way of truth, and they have not prepared the ways to fly to the mountain of myrrh. So the stars are obscured by an intervening cloud. The moon stands, the stars cry out that the moon is falling. The sun obscures them, because nothing of them shines, but is bound up in confusion.

"Whence, O great shepherd named after Christ, offer light to the mountains and the rod to the valleys. Give instructions to the magistrates and discipline to the subjects, spread justice with oil on the mountains and the yoke of obedience on the valleys, mixed with good odors and make straight the paths for them, so they will not appear vile to the Sun of justice. Make your eyes pure, so that your eyes may be everywhere. Water your mind with the pure fountain, so you can shine with the sun and follow the Lamb."

The poor little woman trembles since she speaks in the

sound of words to such a great magistrate. But, O mild Father, the ancient one and wonderful warrior says these things, so hear: "It is directed to you from the highest judge, to root out the heavy and impious tyrants and cast them from you, so they do not stand to your great derision in your presence.

"Also be merciful to public and private troubles, since God does not spurn the wounded or the sorrows of those who tremble."

Whence, O shepherd of sheep, hear these things about this prelate striving in the exhaustion of many things. The Light says: "The mysteries of God know the judgment on everyone according to their merits. But many men wish to hold examination through their envy and disgraceful behavior, but do not know My judgment. Wherefore they inflate their own value like wolves seizing their prey.

"So although a person is worthy to be judged because of his crimes, yet it does not please Me that he desires judgment for himself according to his own decisions. For I do not desire this. But you must judge the case according to the maternal bowels of God's mercy, who does not separate the poor and needy from Himself, since He wishes for mercy rather than sacrifices.

"Now therefore the wicked desire to wash away their wickedness with their own iniquity, but they are lying filthy and deaf in the ditch. Lift them up and aid the weak." [v.A. 1.5]

LETTER TO LUITGARD OF KARLBERG(?)
A LAYWOMAN

O Luitgard, God's creation, arrange your affairs according to your needs, because I do not see your husband's illness lifting before his end. Therefore, beseech, correct, and warn him for the safety of his soul, as I see much darkness in him. May God look upon you, that you may live in eternity. [Pi. 560]

TO HENRY II OF ENGLAND (CA. 1154)

It seems from the tone of the letter that it must have been written early in Henry's career and well before his falling out with Thomas Becket, archbishop of Canterbury, which led eventually to the latter's martyrdom in 1170 and canonization three years later.

To a certain man who holds a certain office, the Lord says: "Yours are the gifts of giving: it is by ruling and defending, protecting and providing, that you may reach Heaven." But a bird, pitch-black, comes to you from the North and says: "You can do whatever you want; so do this and do that; make this excuse and that excuse, for it does not profit you to have regard to Justice; for if you always consult her, you are not the master but the slave."

You however, should not listen to the Thief advising you like this, who in the first age stripped you of great glory, when from dust you were made a beautiful form and received the vital spark of life. Pay more attention to your Father who created you, since your mind is well-intentioned, so you willingly do good unless you are overborne by the squalid habits of others and become entangled in them for a time. Dear son of God, flee this and call on your Father with all your might, as He gladly reaches out His hand to help you. Now may you live forever and dwell in eternal felicity. [Pi. 556]

To Abbess Hazzecha of Krauftal
(ca. 1160–61)

Krauftal was in the diocese of Strasbourg. Hazzecha wrote to Hildegard at least twice about her difficulties in preserving order in her convent and her desire to lay aside the burdens of office for what she saw as a more spiritual way of life.

Who sees all, says: "You have eyes for observing and looking all about you. Where you see dirt, wash it; and what is dry, make green. And make the spices you have release their perfume. Now, had you no eyes you would be able to excuse yourself. But you have eyes. So why do you not use them to look around? But you are eloquent in rationality. Many times you judge others in things for which you do not wish to be judged. But sometimes you say the things that you bring out wisely.

"Mind therefore that you carry your burden properly and collect good works in the purse of your heart lest you fail, since in the solitary life that you seem to be asking for you will not be able to be at peace on account of the fluctuation of irresolute behavior. So then the outcome will be much worse than your beginning and still as grievous as casting the burden away. Imitate the turtledove in chastity; but administer the chosen vineyard diligently so that you can look on God with a pure and righteous face." [v.A. 2.159R]

To the Nuns at Rupertsberg (ca. 1170)

O daughters who have followed the footsteps of Christ in loving chastity and who have chosen me as your mother, poor little woman that I am, in humble subjection on account of supernal exaltation, not from me, but from the divine showing I say to you from my maternal heart: "This place, that is to say the place of the repose of the relics of blessed Rupert the confessor, to whose protection you have fled, I found in manifest miracles through the will of God in the sacrifice of praise, and I came to it with permission of my masters and freely won it for myself and all who should come after me with divine help.

"But later, through the advice of God, I went to the mount of Blessed Disibod, from which I had seceded with permission, and concluded my proposal before all who dwelt there: that is to say, that our place and the proceeds of the donations of our place be not tied but set free from them, while seeking there salvation of our souls and the keeping of the strict rule, as was useful and opportune. And all conceded this freedom to me, and it was guaranteed in writing. And all those who saw, heard, and understood it, both great and small, had great goodwill toward these things, since they had been confirmed in writing by the will of God. All who adhered to God learned and heard these things, and in goodwill affirmed the matter, fulfilling and defending it, inasmuch as they understood it to be that blessing that God gave to Jacob and Israel.

"But oh, what great sorrow will you, my daughters, have after the death of their mother, since they will no more be able to suck her breasts and thus with sorrow and groans for a long time will tearfully say: 'Alas, alas, we would eagerly suck the breasts of our mother, if she were now present with us!' Wherefore, O daughters of God, I warn you to have charity among yourselves, just as I, your mother, have advised you since my childhood, inasmuch as you may be the brightest light among the angels on account of your benevolence and most vigorous in your strength, just as your father Benedict taught you.

"May the Holy Spirit grant you His gifts, because after my end you will no more hear my voice; but my voice will never be forgotten among you, since it will often sound among you in love.

"The hearts of my daughters, panting and sighing for heavenly things, now burn for the sadness that they feel for their mother. Afterward they will shine in most clear and sparkling light through the grace of God and be most valiant soldiers in the house of God. Whence, if anyone in this company of my daughters wishes to cause discord and division of this house and its spiritual discipline, may the gift of the Holy Spirit avert it from her heart. For if, scorning God, that were to be done, the hand of the Lord would cut it down before all the people, since it is right that it should be confounded.

"Wherefore, O daughters, live in this place in which you have chosen to fight for God with all devotion and stability, so you will earn your heavenly reward in it." [v.A. 2.195R]

To Her Brother Hugo (ca. 1170)

The names of seven of Hildegard's siblings are known. Drutwin was the eldest brother, Hugo was precentor of Mainz Cathedral, and Roricus was a canon of Tholey in the Saar region. Of the four sisters known by name—Irmengard, Odilia, Jutta, and Clementia—the last was a nun at Rupertsberg. Hugo acted as secretary to Hildegard for a short time after the death of Volmar. The circumstances of this letter are unknown.

The Church often reports extraordinary things, and thus from time to time they are exaggerated beyond the truth and become ludicrous. Whence I advise you not to accuse your brother Roricus unjustly in your heart, and not to entangle your mind in the wanderings of depraved words about him, because God knows that you do not act rightly in this.

Take care that your Lord does not blame you for this anger of yours and other similar things. May God pardon you for all your sins. (v.A. 2.208)

To the Abbot of Himmerod(?) (ca. 1171)

O mild father, concerning the various happenings to men and what the future might bring them, I am not accustomed to speak, since I, a poor and unlearned little woman, cannot know anything but what I am taught in true vision. But I shall willingly pray for that woman that she be guided in body and soul by God's grace and made glad by an heir worthy of God.

And I heard these words in a true vision of my soul: "You, O man, beware lest you climb higher than your abilities will allow, but in all your doings embrace the most sweet mother of virtues, that is, Discretion, and be guided by her in all things and you will not fall. For the shepherd who wields the rod of correction without discretion is not pleasing to God and will not be loved by his flock but rather hated."

Good father, rule your sheep with mercy, imitating God, who prefers mercy to sacrifices, and take care that all your works are performed in the true humility in which the true Sun, the Son of God, descended from the stronghold of the

Father, into the womb of the Virgin, so that you may live with Him forever. [v.A. 2.118]

HILDEGARD TO POPE ALEXANDER (CA. 1173)

The dispute alluded to here arose from the fact that when Volmar died in 1173, the Rupertsberg nuns were refused their selection of a new provost (as promised to them in a charter of archbishop Arnold of Mainz in 1158 and confirmed by Frederick Barbarossa in 1163) from Disibodenberg by the abbot. The dispute was later settled in Hildegard's favor when the monk Godfrey of Disibodenberg, one of the authors of Hildegard's *Vita*, was appointed. Alexander III, though elected in 1159, spent most of his papacy opposed to Frederick Barbarossa and his succession of three antipopes. They were finally reconciled in 1177 by the Treaty of Venice.

O supreme and glorious person, who was first constituted by the word of God, through which all Creation, rational and irrational in its kind, was made, to you especially the Word has given the keys of the Kingdom of Heaven, that is, the power to bind and loose, through putting on the garment of his humanity.

You also, most excellent Father, are the pattern of all spiritual persons, who sound the trumpet of the justice of God in the Church, which shines, surrounded with various ornaments, while others offer to others good examples in imitating the life of the saints. And if they act righteously they attribute it not to themselves but to God, and rejoice concerning their good followers, imitating the saints before, who gave their flesh and strengthened themselves with manifest victory of the heavenly army fighting against the vices of the Devil, and with goodwill looked on God, like the angels.

So you, also, O mild Father, imitate that benign father who joyfully took up the son returning penitent to him and killed the fatted calf for him. And imitate the one who washed with wine the wounds, mired with dust, of the man wounded by robbers. This shows harshness of correction and the piety of mercy. And be a morning star, which goes before the day's sun, to the Church, which for a long time has been mired with the dust of schism, lacking the light of God's justice. And you therefore, in accordance with the zeal of God, reprove and anoint the penitents with the oil of mercy, since God prefers mercy to sacrifices.

Now O most mild Father, I and my sisters bend our knees before your paternal piety, praying that you deign to look upon the need of this poor little woman, since we are now in great sadness, because the abbot of Disibodenberg and his brothers deny us our privilege of election. We always had this privilege and always took great care to retain it lest it be in any way taken from us, since if God-fearing monks are not allowed to us such as we ask for, all feeling of religion will be destroyed in us.

Whence, my lord, help us for the sake of God, so that we can have the one we elected, or freely ask for and receive others, wherever we can, who will look after us and our interests according to God.

Now again, we ask you, most pious Father, not to despise our petition and these messengers coming to you, who, advised through our faithful friend, have turned to us, and do what they seek to obtain from you, so that at the end of this life, which already declines to evening, you may reach the never-failing light and hear the sweet voice of the Lord: "Well done, good and faithful servant, because thou hast been faithful over a few things, I will place thee over many things: enter thou into the joy of the Lord" [*Mt.* 25:21]. Therefore incline the ears of your piety to our prayers and be to us and to them the clear day, so that from the indulgence of your generosity we may rejoice together in the Lord, in as much as you may ever rejoice in eternal felicity. [v.A. 1.10]

FROM HILDEGARD'S LETTER TO THE MONK GUIBERT OF GEMBLOUX (CA. 1175)

Guibert, from the monastery of Gembloux in Flanders, first started writing to Hildegard in 1175 and paid a visit to Rupertsberg the following year. When Godfrey of Disibodenberg died in 1176, Hildegard procured the services of her brother Hugo from Mainz, together with a canon from St. Stephen's in Mainz. Guibert was invited to Rupertsberg in 1177 and shortly thereafter both Mainz clerics were carried off by a fever, leaving Guibert to step into their shoes. He remained at Rupertsberg until 1180, when he was recalled to Gembloux.

God works where He will for the glory of His name and not for that of earthly man. And I have always had a trembling fear, since I have never felt secure in my own abilities. But I stretch out my hands to God, so that like a feather, which lacks all solidity of strength and flies on the wind, I may be sustained by Him. And the things that I see I cannot know perfectly while I am in my bodily form with an invisible soul, since man is lacking in these two things.

From my infancy, when my bones and nerves and veins were as yet imperfect, I have always enjoyed the gift of this vision in my soul, up to the present time, when I am now more than seventy years old. Indeed my spirit, when God wills, ascends aloft to the heights of the firmament and to the changing aspects of different climes and spreads itself through diverse peoples though they are in far-off regions and places remote from me. And as I see things in this way I perceive them in the changing clouds and other creatures. And I do not hear them with my bodily ears, nor with the thoughts of my heart, nor do I perceive them through a combination of my five senses, but ever in my soul, with my external eyes open, so that I never suffer debilitating ecstasy. And I am continually constrained by illness and hedged about with heavy pains that threaten to be my undoing. But until now God has sustained me.

The light that I see has no position but is much brighter than the cloud that surrounds the sun, and I can discern no height or depth nor extension in it. And it has been named for me the Shadow of the Living Light. And as the sun, moon, and stars appear reflected in water, so the scriptures, writings, virtues, and certain works of men taking form in it are reflected for me.

I retain the memory of whatever I see or learn in such vision for a long time, so that whatever I once see or hear I remember. And I see and hear and know at one and the same time; and in a flash that which I learn, I know. And what I do not see, I do not know, since I am not learned. And the things which I write, I see and hear in that vision, and I do not put down any other words than those I hear, and I offer whatever I hear in the vision in unpolished Latin, since I have not been taught to write in the vision as philosophers write. And the words which I see and hear in the vision are not like the words that sound from the mouth of man, but like a sparkling flame and a cloud moved by the pure air. I cannot in any way ascertain the form of the light, just as I cannot properly discern the sphere of the sun.

And in that light, occasionally and infrequently I see another light, which I have been told is the Living Light, and I am even less able to say how I see it than the first, but while I behold it, all sadness and all pain is lifted from my memory, so that I feel like a carefree young girl and not the old woman that I am. [v.A. 2.103R]

Select Bibliography

HILDEGARD'S WORKS

Scivias

EDITION:

Führkötter, Adelgundis, and Angela Carlevaris. *Hildegardis—Scivias*. In Corpus Christianorum: Continuatio Mediaevalis (CCCM), vol. 43, 43A. Turnhout, Belgium: Brepols, 1978.

ENGLISH TRANSLATION:

Hart, Columba, and Jane Bishop. *Hildegard of Bingen: Scivias*. The Classics of Western Spirituality. New York: Paulist Press, 1990.

Book of Life's Merits (Liber vitae meritorum)

EDITION:

Carlevaris, Angela. *Hildegardis—Liber vitae meritorum*, In CCCM. vol. 90. Turnhout, Belgium: Brepols, 1995.

Book of Divine Works (Liber divinorum operum)

EDITIONS:

In *Patrologia Latina*, edited by J.-P. Migne. Vol. 197.

to be replaced by:

Derolez, Albert and Peter Dronke. *Hildegardis—Liber divinorum operum*. In CCCM. Turnhout, Belgium: Brepols, forthcoming, 1996.

Natural History (Physica)

EDITIONS:

In *Patrologia Latina*, edited by J.-P. Migne. Vol. 197.

179

to be replaced by:

Müller, Irmgard. *Hildegardis—Physica*. In CCCM. Turnhout, Belgium: Brepols, forthcoming.

Causes and Cures (Causae et Curae)

EDITION:

Kaiser, Paul. *Hildegardis Causae et curae*. Leipzig: Teubner, 1903.

Symphonia (Symphonia armonie celestium revelationum)

EDITION AND ENGLISH TRANSLATION:

Newman, Barbara. *Hildegard of Bingen: Symphonia*. Ithaca: Cornell University Press, 1988.

Play of the Virtues (Ordo virtutum)

EDITION:

in Dronke, Peter. *Poetic Individuality in the Middle Ages*. Oxford: Clarendon Press, 1970.

PERFORMANCE EDITION:

Davidson, Audrey. *The "Ordo virtutum" of Hildegard*. Kalamazoo: Medieval Institute, 1985.

Life of St. Disibod and Life of St. Rupert (Vita S. Ruperti; Vita S. Disibodi)

EDITION:

in *Patrologia Latina*, edited by J.-P. Migne. Vol. 197

Correspondence

EDITIONS:

Pitra, Jean-Baptiste. *Sanctae Hildegardis Opera*. Analecta Sacra, vol. 8. Monte Cassino, 1882.

van Acker, L. *Hildegardis Bingensis—Epistolarium*, vol. 1 (letters 1–90), CCCM 91, and vol. 2 (letters 91–250), CCCM 91A. Turnhout, Belgium: Brepols, 1991, 1993.

(Further volumes, containing the remaining letters and many of Hildegard's minor works, are in preparation.)

ENGLISH TRANSLATION:

Baird, Joseph, and Radd Ehrman. *The Letters of Hildegard of Bingen*, vol. 1. New York: Oxford University Press, 1995. (A translation of the letters in van Acker's volume 1; other volumes are planned.)

Life of Hildegard by Godfrey and Theodorich
(Vita Sanctae Hildegardis)

EDITION:

Klaes, Monika *Vita Sanctae Hildegardis*. CCCM 126. Turnhout: Brepols, 1993.

(German translations of Hildegard's major works [sometimes abridged] are published by Otto Müller Verlag, Salzburg.)

SECONDARY WORKS

Dronke, Peter. *Women Writers of the Middle Ages: A Critical Study of Texts from Perpetua (died 203) to Marguerite Porete (died 1310)*. Cambridge: Cambridge University Press, 1984.

Flanagan, Sabina. *Hildegard of Bingen: A Visionary Life*, London and New York: Routledge, 1989

————. *Hildegard von Bingen*, in "German Writers and Works of the Early Middle Ages: 800–1170." *Dictionary of Literary Biography*, vol. 148. New York: Gale, 1995

Newman, Barbara *Sister of Wisdom: St. Hildegard's Theology of the Feminine*. Berkeley: University of California Press, 1987.

Schrader, Marianna, and Adelgundis Führkötter. *Die Echtheit des Schrifttums der hl. Hildegard von Bingen*. Quellenkritische Untersuchungen. Cologne: Böhlau-Verlag, 1956.

BIBLIOGRAPHY

Lauter, Werner *Hildegard-Bibliographie I, II*. Alzey: Rheinhessische Druckwerkstätte, 1970, 1983. (A third volume is in preparation). (See also bibliographies in the secondary works above.)

SELECT DISCOGRAPHY

A Feather on the Breath of God: Sequences and Hymns by Abbess Hildegard of Bingen. Gothic Voices. LP/MC/CD: Hyperion A/KA/CDA 66039 (1981).

Geistliche Musik des Mittelalters und der Renaissance. Instrumental-kreise Helga Weber. TELDEC LP 66.22387 (1980).

Gesänger der hl. Hildegard von Bingen. Schola der Benediktinerinnen-abtei St. Hildegard in Eibingen. LP/MC: Psallite 242.040479/ 242 (1979).

Hildegard von Bingen: Ordo virtutum. Sequentia, LP: Deutsche Harmonia Mundi 20.395/96; CD: CDS 7492498; MC: 77051-4-RG (1982). With an English translation by Peter Dronke.

Hildegard von Bingen: Symphoniae (Geistliche Gesänge). Sequentia. LP: Deutsche Harmonia Mundi 1C 067-1999761; CD: CDC 7492512; MC 77020-4-RG (1983).

Hildegard von Bingen und ihre Zeit. (Songs by Hildegard and Abelard). Ensemble für frühe Musik Augsburg. Christophorus CD 74584 (1990).

Jouissance: Hildegard and Abelard. Viriditas. CD Spectrum Publications, Richmond, Victoria, Australia 3121 (1994).

The Lauds of Saint Ursula. Early Music Institute, University of Indiana. CD: Focus 911 (1991).

Index

Adam, 47, 77, 109, 125; creation of, 20–21, 53, 64, 70–71, 106, 113–14, 121; disobedience of, 59, 138, 140, 144, 159, 165; fall of, 12, 14, 15, 21, 55, 108, 159, 170; expelled from Paradise, 108, 156. *See also* Eve

Alexander III, Pope, 174–75

Angels, 13, 26, 46, 63, 86, 134, 163, 175; orders of, 143, 159; praise God, 57, 71, 76; radiance of, 79, 172

Animals, 106, 159, 165; in Paradise, 63; before the Flood, 109; in purgatory 47–48, 54; terrestrial: calf, 175; dog, 53, 98–99; earthworm, 101; elephant, 137; goat, 58, 137; mole, 99; mouse, 99–100; ram, 137; sheep, 160, 174; snake, 52, 56, 100–101; unicorn, 96–97; whale, 73; used figuratively: hart 114, 137, 152, 162; goat, 47; lion, 139; sheep, 85, 168; unicorn, 47; wolf, 85, 162, 168; symbolizing historical periods, 34–35

Antichrist, 34, 35, 36–37, 85–87

Apostles, 75, 82, 84. *See also* Saints: Paul

Arnold of Mainz, Archbishop, 174

Bamberg, 6

Baptism, 23–24

Bassum, 6, 160

Bernard of Clairvaux, 1, 154–57

Bible, 36; Gospels, 1, 9, 26, 38, 62, 155; John, 71–72, 159; Matthew, 158, 176; Luke, 30; 2 Thessalonians, 86; Genesis, 62, 72–74; Isaiah, 17, 73, 143; Job, 159; Baruch, 45; Psalms, 9, 57, 78, 155, 165; Canticles, 146; Apocalypse, 159

Birds, 53, 56, 65–66, 95–96, 169; creation of, 73, 165, 169. *See also* Dove; Eagle

Christian of Mainz, Archbishop, 7

Church (*Ecclesia*), 1, 24–25, 74–76, 85, 128, 136; as bride of Christ, 26–29, 34; as spiritual mother, 24

183

Circumcision, 23, 47
Cologne, 6, 128
Communion, 27–29, 128
Conception, 106–7, 110, 119
Confession: to priest, 43
Conrad III, Emperor, 11
Creation: God's work of, 18, 49, 50, 56, 70, 73, 74–77, 81–82, 125–26, 140. *See also* Adam: creation of; Eve: creation of; Microcosm
Crucifixion, 26–29, 121, 138
Cuno of Disibodenberg, Abbot, 11, 161, 162

Desire, 110–11, 114
Devil: and Adam, 13–15, 18, 21, 30; and Disibod, 151; and Elisabeth of Schönau, 166; and Richardis, 164; and Rupert, 134; and Ursula 129, 131; hates dogs, 98; renounced by mortals, 41, 59, 175; seduces mankind, 45, 55, 123, 126, 139, 156, 157, 165, 170; in *Play of the Virtues*, 140–41; vanquished, 31, 47, 51, 63, 129–30, 139, 141; in the Last Days, 83, 86–87. *See also* Lucifer
Diet, 112–13, 114–15
Disibodenberg, 5, 6, 127, 150–53, 160, 171
Dove, 73, 76, 131, 132, 136, 171
Dreams, 111, 143–44
Dronke, Peter, 5

Eagle, 16, 63, 156
Earth: before, the Flood, 69, 71, 82; qualities of, 101, 105–6;

relationship to mankind, 52–53
Eibingen, 6
Elements: of the world, 37, 48–49, 50–51, 66, 85, 129, 165; present in humans, 107–8, 109–10. *See also* Microcosm
Elisabeth of Schönau, 164–66
Enoch and Elijah, 85–86
Eugenius III, Pope, 5, 11, 155, 167–69
Eve, 79, 130, 157–58; creation of, 70, 79, 113–14, 126; transgression of, 14–15, 27, 96, 123, 124, 125, 126. *See also* Adam

Fish, 91–92, 94–95, 165
Flood (Deluge), 84, 108
Frederick I (Barbarossa), Emperor, 1, 6, 174

Gebeno of Eberbach, Prior, xi
Gems. *See* Precious stones
Glan, river, 92, 149
Godfrey of Disibodenberg, 4, 7, 160, 174, 176
Guibert of Gembloux, 7, 176, 177

Hartwig of Bremen, Archbishop, 161–64
Hazzecha of Krauftal, Abbess, 170–71
Helenger of Disibodenberg, Abbot, 6, 127, 142, 175
Henry of Mainz, Archbishop, 11, 167
Henry II, King of England, 169–70
Hermann of Stahleck, Court Palatine, 162, 163

Hildegard of Bingen: birthplace of, 5; death of, 7; education of, 3–4, 19, 155–56, 178; family of, 2–3, 173, 176; illnesses of, 4, 6, 10, 11, 156, 177; personality of, 4–5, 154, 166; preaching of, 6, 7; as prophet, 2, 19, 36; visions of, 4, 8–10, 87–88, 155, 163–64, 177–78; works of: *Book of Divine Works*, 6, 7, 62–88, 142; *Book of Life's Merits*, 6, 39–61, 81; *Causes and Cures*, 6, 104–19; *Life of St. Disibod*, 6, 127, 146–53; *Life of St. Rupert*, 6, 142–46; *Natural History*, 6, 89–103; *Scivias*, 5, 6, 8–38, 39, 80, 120, 155, 160; *Play of the Virtues*, 120, 139–41; *Symphonia*, 6, 120–41; Correspondence, 4–5, 154–78

Hördt, 6

Humoral theory, 107–8. *See also* Illnesses

Illnesses, 111–13, 115–19, 144–45, 152, 153, 169; and animals, 97–101; and birds, 95–96; and fish, 94–95; and gems, 93–94; and metals, 101–103; and plants; 89–91; and trees, 92–93

Incarnation, 47, 53, 65, 84, 157, 165–66, 174; foreshadowing of, 17–18, 20, 75; Mary's role in, 123–25; no lessening of power in, 44; overcomes death/ the Devil, 18, 75, 139, 141; represented at baptism, 23; restores tenth order of angels, 71–72; and salvation, 77–79

John the Baptist, 22

Jutta of Spanheim, 3, 5

Krauftal, 6

Lamb of God (Christ), 63, 65, 74, 129, 131, 159, 166, 168

Life of St. Hildegard (*Vita Hildegardis*), 7, 160, 174

Last Judgment, 37–38, 42, 61, 69, 83, 85

Love (*Caritas*), 62–66, 79–82

Lucifer, 54, 67–68; fall of, 12–13, 28, 71, 82, 122, 159. *See also* Devil

Ludwig of St. Eucharius, Abbot, 87

Metz, 6

Main, river, 6

Marriage, 25–26, 29, 74; of the Church, 26–27, 29; celestial, 128, 138–39, 158–59

Martyrs, 60, 65, 127. *See also* St. Ursula

Metals, 101–3

Microcosm, humanity as, 64, 66–67, 71, 109–10

Monastic life, 25, 61, 73, 133, 146, 151

Music, 31, 40, 42, 46, 60, 72, 129, 134, 166

Nahe, river, 91–92

Paradise, 14, 15–16, 47, 108

Penance, 43, 51, 54, 57, 59, 67, 86

Plants, 60, 89–91, 146, 165; in Paradise, 16, 97; and the

Flood, 84; and diet, 112; and Disibod, 132, 134, 150, 152; and Mary, 124; and Rupert, 143, 146

Precious stones, 16, 38, 68, 83, 122, 123, 138, 166; amber, 60; crystal, 60, 127; emerald, 59, 93–94; jacinth, 137; pearls, 129; sapphire, 44, 128, 129, 133; sardonyx, 137; topaz, 133; in heavenly Jerusalem, 134

Prophets, 36, 57, 75, 80–81, 139–40, 143

Purgatory, 16, 42–43, 47–48

Reason, 64–65, 80, 122, 128

Rhine, river, 6, 145, 149

Richardis of Stade, 3, 5, 6, 8, 11, 160–64

Richardis of Stade, Marchioness (mother of the above), 3, 161, 163

Rupertsberg, 6, 7, 120, 142, 160, 171, 176

Satan. See Devil; Lucifer

Schism, 6, 175

Seculars (laity), 25, 59, 73

Serpent (in Paradise), 14, 157

Son of Perdition. See Antichrist

Saints: Boniface, 127; Disibod, 127–28, 131–33, 146–53; Eucharius, 135–36; John the Evangelist, 131; Maximin, 136–38; Paul, 65, 86, 158, 160; Rupert, 133–35, 142–46, 171; Ursula, 128–31, 165

Theodorich of Echternach, 4, 160

Tengswich of Andernach, 157

Trees, 54–55, 74, 92–93, 137, 156, 165; in Paradise, 14

Trinity, 17, 20, 22–23, 47, 71

Trier, 5, 6, 87, 120, 135, 136, 155

Virgin Mary, 18, 20, 22, 53, 71–72, 75, 84, 130; chosen by Christ, 44, 47; and Eve, 78–79, 123–26, 130

Virginity, 44, 61, 73, 130, 138, 158–59, 164

Vices, 31, 40–41; bestiality, 51–52; covetousness, 53; discord, 54; falsity 47; pride, 49; worldly love, 43; worldly sadness, 54–55, 56–57

Virtues, 29–31, 33, 54, 139–41, 166; chastity and continence, 73–74, 141; discretion, 31–32, 174; heavenly love, 41; heavenly joy, 55–56, 57; humility, 79, 81; mercy, 162; peace, 79; exemplified in Christ, 32–33. See also Love; Reason; Wisdom

Volmar of Disibodenberg, 3–4, 5, 8, 10–11, 156; death of, 7, 87–88, 173, 174

Weather, 104–5

Werden, 6

Wezelin, nephew of Hildegard, 88

Wisdom (Sapientia), 50, 63, 79–81, 84, 120–21, 137, 146

Zwiefalten, 7

Plate 3.

Plate 4.